THE RED RIVER VALLEY *in* ARKANSAS

Gateway to the Southwest

ROBIN COLE-JETT

THE History PRESS

Published by The History Press
Charleston, SC 29403
www.historypress.net

First published 2014

Manufactured in the United States

ISBN 978.1.62619.173.0

Library of Congress CIP data applied for.

Notice: The information in this book is true and complete to the best of our knowledge. It is offered without guarantee on the part of the author or The History Press. The author and The History Press disclaim all liability in connection with the use of this book.

Contents

Acknowledgements

Since the turn of this century, I have been documenting the history of the Red River Valley, from its source in Palo Duro Canyon all the way down to the Mississippi River. The small website I started back in 2001—based on a newsletter I had begun to publish earlier—has now grown into a database of sorts for Red River history. When I was contacted to write a book about my favorite topic of conversation, I jumped at the chance. I feel so very fortunate to share with readers my never-ending fascination with this body of water and the cultures that surround it.

I specifically chose to focus on the Great Bend region—southwestern Arkansas—because I fell in love with Fulton. The Red River does not host many towns that sit along its banks anymore, as most settlements have fallen victim to flash floods, high water, railroads and highways. While most towns have succumbed long ago to a more modern age, that is not the case for Fulton (or its downriver sister, Garland City). Old maps still show locations of bygone river towns, like Laynesport, Rocky Comfort, La Grange and Lost Prairie, but only Fulton and Garland still retain their locations along the river, where steamships docked and ferries crossed, where inhabitants carried on even if they had to slosh through a foot or more of water. I admire these stalwarts of time passed, and although the towns no longer reflect their former glories, they inhabit the keen sense of place that makes me so interested in the history and geography of the Red River Valley.

Writing this book would not have been possible without so many wonderful, dedicated people. The archivists, librarians and historians at the

Dallas Public Library, Arkansas Historical Commission and Southwestern Arkansas Regional Archives made my research work a true joy. My coworkers at North Central Texas College gave me much encouragement, as did my friends and family, especially my husband, Raymond; son, David; and mother, Barbara. Finally, I wish to thank the wonderful folks at The History Press.

With this book, I hope readers will discover their own enthrallment with the Red River.

Introduction

Sam Williams, an emigrant from Kentucky who arrived in southwestern Arkansas as an infant in 1838, lived along the Red River during his entire youth, first in Fulton and then in Washington, where he learned the newspaper trade at the *Washington Telegraph*. He wrote about his experiences in a memoir titled *Printer's Devil*—the moniker for a printer's apprentice. During his youth in Fulton, he watched the Red River at flood stage; his lasting impression of this "stupendous expanse of water" was that "its banks were full to the top of very reddish, very muddy-looking water." His description, while not very poetic, did include another, very important detail: "Upon the bank of the stream, at the ferry landing in Fulton, sat a man in his shirtsleeves, washing a pair of stockings in this red and dirty water as it swept by him in a ceaseless current." He saw the river not just as an obstacle to overcome or as a geographic feature to be feared. Unlike a naturalist or a scientist who focuses on hard data, Williams viewed the river as a historian would: a conduit for human interaction. It is within this context that the Red River in southwestern Arkansas should be defined.

When seen through the lens of humanity, rivers have served several distinct functions throughout much of history: as barriers, geographic boundaries and intermediaries for commerce and relationships. The Great Bend of the Red River definitely encompassed all three. The river barred people from their destinations, whether during floods or periods of drought, and presented a major obstacle in the growth of overland transportation, as trains and automobiles needed efficient and safe methods to cross the water. At one point, the river functioned as the border between the United States and Mexico, and it still marks the legal boundary between the states of Texas and Arkansas as it flows eastward toward the Index Line. Lastly, the river acted as an intermediary between the people who have called or still call southwestern Arkansas home and their environment—from the ferries that carried them across the stream to the boats laden with produce and gadgets that introduced adults and children alike to a wider world.

The past has put the river to good use. The Red River was America's westernmost stream in which steamship activity became an important factor in building the economy. It was also one of the few rivers in America where waterway navigation was completely abandoned when the railroads appeared. The Red River is the thread that weaves the history of southwestern Arkansas together. This is why I have refrained from an extensive, detailed writing of histories about prominent people, congregations, companies, towns or schools. The stories of the rich and famous and their institutions have been recorded and retold ad nauseam and can be found in many historical journals, commemorative books and other tomes about the region. While notable people and places are of importance and do get mentioned, the focus of this story is on the relationship between the river and the people who surround it. Quite often, I have learned that the accounts of the regular, salt-of-the-earth kinds of men and women are the fodder for the most illustrative histories. In an account about how a river has affected its people, the everyday Joe or Jane provides a perspective of how it is to live with the river and not how to conquer or even negate it, as so many of the more prominent citizens have done.

As a historian who teaches a college survey course in American history, I have discovered quite the remarkable thing about southwestern Arkansan history: it mirrors the overarching stories in the greater American narrative in most, if not all, ways. Themes that have a tendency to appear throughout American history—Manifest Destiny, Jeffersonian democracy, post–Civil War malaise, incorporation and the southern cotton empire—are well represented in the retelling of southwestern Arkansas' past. A history professor could literally use just the Great Bend region to illustrate the outcomes of major historical events after the founding of the United States. Studying the four counties that surround the Red River—Miller, Little River, Lafayette and Hempstead—provides insight into American history as a whole.

The Red River may not be as grand as the Mississippi, as integral as the Ohio, as scenic as the Hudson or as well explored as the Missouri, but it is the path on which much of Arkansas' history was formed.

Chapter 1

Along the River

Inhabitants and Settlers

The Red River is, by all accounts, not the most impressive body of water in the United States. While it empties as a formidable delta into the mighty Mississippi in eastern Louisiana, it has its beginnings as a puddle of spring water in the arid landscape of the Caprock, a geological fissure that separates the plains of northwestern Texas. For at least half of its 1,360-mile run, the river does not yield much water, and its shifting banks do not easily lend themselves to permanent settlements. Most Americans who tried to settle along the river found their villages swept away by torrential floods or dry-docked by thousands of oxbow lakes that formed practically overnight. To European Americans, the river often proved wild and unpredictable.

One may wish to underestimate the Red River Valley's importance in western history, but it is not the size of the water that matters; it is the geography through which it travels that makes the Red River of the South such an interesting study of human interactions. The river runs roughly from west to east geographically and from east to west historically. Along its banks, the plantation culture of the Old South gave way to the cattle trails of the Wild West. The agricultural kingdoms of the Caddoan peoples defined the eastern part of the river, whereas the nomadic empires of the Wichitas, Comanches and Kiowas ruled the western prairies. Majestic virgin pine forests turn to gnarly post oak copses in the Cross Timbers before the landscape becomes treeless in the staked plains. In Louisiana and Arkansas, the Red River is an eastern body, with locks and levies controlling the flow. In Oklahoma and Texas, the river is purely a western stream, dry and sandy

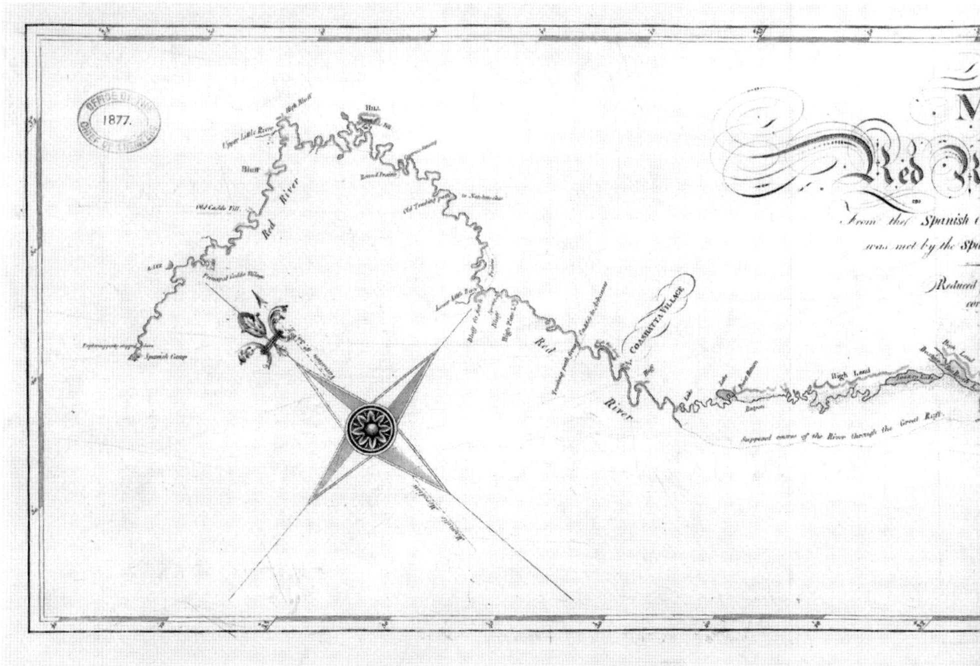

The Freeman and Custis expedition of 1806, ordered by President Thomas Jefferson after the Louisiana Purchase, produced one of the earliest maps of the Red River. *Courtesy Library of Congress.*

most of the year. The river is a constant juxtaposition of the South and West, and it is in Arkansas where the two regional distinctions collide, forming what nineteenth-century surveyors deemed the Great Southwest—and what we now call the "Old Southwest."

The Red River enters the state of Arkansas southwest of Foreman, running an easterly course. Just after the Little River merges with it, the river suddenly plunges due south, making a dramatic bend at today's Fulton. This turn was known far and wide as the "Great Bend" of the Red River. The stream makes many more bends as it meanders south through the state, sometimes changing its course either to the north or the west as it slithers its way toward the ocean. The channel cuts many unnecessary turns through the sandy soil, marking the Red River with a plethora of oxbow lakes, or river cut-offs. The circuitous way the Red River flows has been often described as "tortuous"; for example, the southern and western boundaries of Miller County are each about 50 miles in length, but the county's eastern boundary, marked by the Red River, is over 150 miles long.[1]

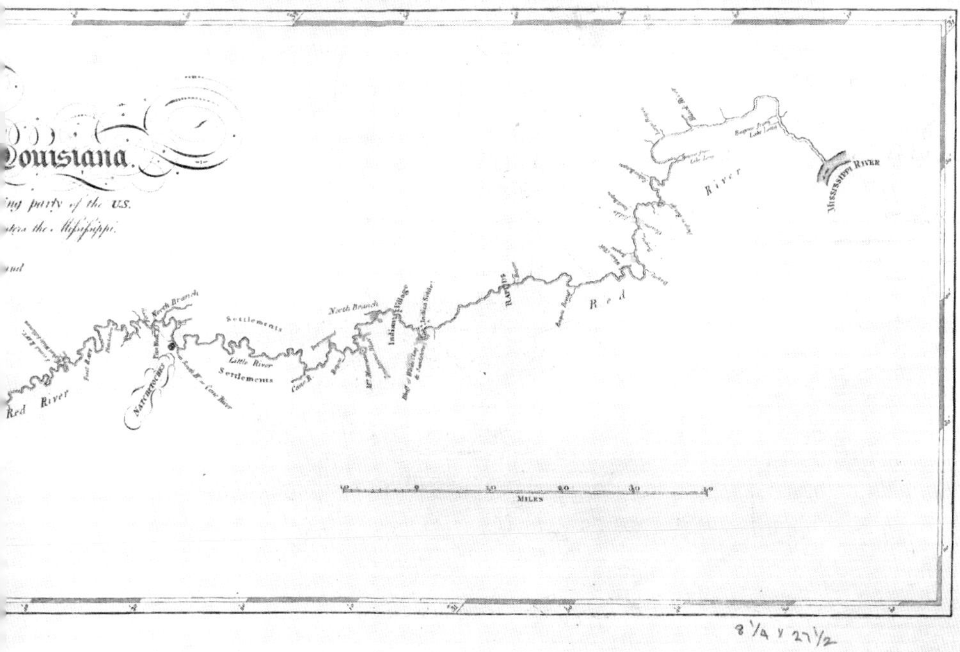

Near the Louisiana line, the Sulphur River merges with the Red. Then, past Shreveport, the Red gradually flows southeast through Louisiana. After a series of locks and dams constructed by the U.S. Army Corps of Engineers, the Red River mingles waters with the Atchafalaya River, and a small, tightly controlled stream—a mere remnant of the former massive wetlands of the lower Red River—empties into the mighty Mississippi.

The rich alluvial soils that flank the stream yield some of the most fertile ground in the state, suitable for growing cotton, corn and wheat. The French even gushed that tobacco and indigo planting might be viable.[2] Within the river valley, swaths of prairie grasses grow from loamy deposits of mostly clay, gypsum, sand and gravel. Chalk cliffs can abruptly rise as the land meets with water, and canebrakes surround the low strands. This soft bottomland makes up the Gulf Coastal Plain, created 50 million years ago by a shallow ocean that, as it receded, later formed the Gulf of Mexico. The landscape is mostly flat around the river but rises quite dramatically in the crests between the prairies, where hardwood trees like loblolly pines, oaks, hickories, bois d'arcs, pecans, willows, ash, elms, laurels and cottonwoods predominate. Before European settlement, red cypress trees grew in the river bottoms. With its frequent flooding over the millennia, the Red River has also deposited its fair share of red clay, giving the stream its eponymous hue.

Southwestern Arkansas is fairly mineral rich, with bauxite, lignite coal and petroleum providing the main sources of industrial mining. This might be why, when Englishman G.W. Featherstonhaugh crossed it, he remarked that the river looked "sluggish, muddy, and chocolate-colored."[3] The remarkable soil also lends itself to brick making, a visual remnant of the clay that the aboriginal Indians used to create their remarkable and famed pottery. Today, the main source of regional wealth comes from large-scale farms and timber. Beavers, black bears, elks, deer, coyotes, turkeys, pumas and bison found a home in this ancient landscape, over which the first human inhabitants, the Caddos, ruled for one thousand years.

THE CADDOS IN SOUTHWESTERN ARKANSAS

Because the Caddos did not leave a written record, much of the information about this important nation has been gleaned from oral histories, outsider observations and scientific study. The impression that forms is of a complex, clan-based society with distinct social hierarchies, material wealth, territorial dominancy and language-based kinship.

The Caddoan empire can be traced to about 700 AD. They originated from the Mississippian tradition, a pre-historical group that includes the Choctaws, Chickasaws and Cherokees. Mississippian people shared cultural traits such as relying on agriculture, building funeral mounds, centering their cities on ceremonial temples and basing their families on matrilineal kinship. Though traditional histories tend not to use the term "nation" to describe the ancient homelands of the Caddos, it is nevertheless an apt word, as there were several subgroups of the Caddos who shared a common governmental and religious system and saw their territory as sacrosanct as any British or Spaniard would. To put into perspective, one just has to think of the different groups that make up the British Isles: the Welsh, Cornish, Angles, Saxons and Britons. The Caddos were not dissimilar: they had a nation of disparate groups who shared common beliefs and similar traditions.

Their nation's distinctive subgroups have been likened by anthropologists to chiefdoms or kingdoms. Like most Amerindians of the North American continent, these chiefdoms operated independently from each other. Caddoan

Caddoan artifacts for everyday use have been found during archaeological digs in Miller County. *From the collections of the Arkansas Historical Commission.*

alliances acted therefore more as a confederacy but under a common leadership model. The range of the Caddoan confederacy comprised today's southwestern Arkansas, northwestern Louisiana, northeastern Texas and southeastern Oklahoma. The main chiefdoms were the Natchitoches of northern Louisiana, the Kadohadachos of southern Arkansas and the Hasinais of East Texas. Smaller clans lived among the bigger kingdoms. Related groups around the periphery of the Caddoan confederacy included the Wichitas, Kichais, Taensas and the Quapaws, who figured prominently in early Arkansas history as they lived along the Arkansas River.[4]

The Kadohadachos, which may mean "real chiefs" or "wise king" in the native language (sources differ), lived in clan-based compounds along the Red River in today's southwestern Arkansas. A subgroup of the Kadohadachos were the Upper Nasonis, who also lived along the Great Bend. When disease and war threatened their fellow Caddos, the Kadohadachos welcomed resettlement; for example, the Yatasis, a small Caddoan tribe, set up a small village in the Great Bend area among the Kadohadachos in the late eighteenth century after disease and warfare threatened the survival of their band.[5] Kadohadachoan mound complexes dotted the landscape around the Red River, and their prominent series of mounds provided the name for the first Anglo settlement in the Red River Valley: Mound Prairie. A few mounds can still be seen all around today's Miller, Lafayette and Little River Counties.

The Caddos were a river people. They lived in long, not wide, villages along the Red, Neches, Sabine, Little, Angelina and Ouachita Rivers on cleared land[6] and relied heavily on the seasonal flooding of the streams, which helped them in planting the "three sister crops" of maize, beans and squash. Other harvests included wheat, melons, sunflowers and pumpkins, the latter being used not just for food but also for weaving mats and making baskets. Larger cities centered on ceremonial structures or temples, to which people who lived in smaller villages would travel to trade, celebrate and worship.[7] Depending on where they lived, Caddos built either wooden houses with fireplaces or grass-covered, cone-shaped homes centered around a fire pit. Cultivated fields surrounded their compounds.

The deceased and what to do with them figured prominently in Caddoan culture. The dead were interred in conical earthen mounds, some built in a stair-step fashion that can be likened to the stone pyramids of the Aztecs and Mayans. On top of the mounds sat large, round huts, in which the religious leader dwelled. After the leader died, the temple was burned and rebuilt for the successor.[8] The main spiritual center for the early Caddos was located near today's Spiro, Oklahoma. Until the fifteenth century, this large complex on the Arkansas River was the preferred place of burial for the Caddoan elite and an important ceremonial place, with the center of the mounds used for burial preparations and sacred rituals. Spiro is considered one of four main spiritual sites for the Mississippian people, the others being located in Illinois (the famous Cahokia site), Georgia and Alabama. Excavations of the Spiro mounds have uncovered decorative items made of copper, shell, bone, pottery and pearl. The artifacts reveal a sophisticated trading network throughout the eastern, southern and western Americas. Unfortunately, Spiro's historical treasures were raided by greedy individuals in the 1930s, who excavated the site using steam shovels to sell pieces to unscrupulous collectors and dealers, thus destroying much of the archaeological evidence. Whatever remained was catalogued and shipped to the Smithsonian and other museums on the East Coast. Sadly, many of the artifacts are now held in private collections and remain unknown to researchers. In May 2012, a clay vessel from the Sprio mounds turned up at a Goodwill store in Buffalo, New York. The Goodwill store donated the item to the Caddo Nation.[9]

After the demise of the great ceremonial city, the largest city of the Caddoan confederacy became today's Natchitoches, which sat on a major east–west trade route (later, the Spanish renamed this route the Camino de Real) and was also the convergence of all Caddoan trading paths. From here, Caddos traded their goods with western and eastern tribes, such as the Wichitas and Comanches in the west, the Quapaws in the east and the Jumanjos in the southwest. The main Caddoan exports were pottery, made of red and brown clay and decorated with deep striations, animal heads or inlaid geometric designs; pelts; leather; and strong bows, manufactured from the pliable but hard wood of the bois d'arc tree, also known as the Osage Orange.[10] The Caddos also traded salt, gleaned from the salt marshes just east of present-day Fulton and underground caves. Mounds, middens and sherds have led archaeologists to the conclusion that the salt marshes generated a lot of activity, pre-European contact, and may have been located on an extensive and well-defined trading route.[11] The most prominent salt mine lay in today's Little River County, at Cerro Gordo (also known as Pauly's Cave), where a chance discovery of a partial flintlock pistol from the sixteenth century by R.F. Bolster hinted at early European trade in southwestern Arkansas.[12]

The Caddos' head religious leader was called the *Xinesi*, a man (at times, a woman) who lived inside the temple that was erected on top of the ceremonial mound. His role was to be the spiritual leader of his people. He also kept the spiritual fire in the temple lit. He devoted most of his time to meditation, contemplation and guidance. He was the main conduit for the Caddoan god *Ahahayo* and communicated the god's will to the people. *Xinesi* lived an inward life; as his utmost role was to seek out the spiritual world, he did not engage in labor of any sort and was carried on a litter, even for short distances. He may have also been the king or chief of his tribe; European accounts suggest a military role, and great deference was paid to him. A small contingent of nobles, called the *Caddi*, governed each of the villages. Sixteenth-century Spanish texts named the Caddo king/chief *Cacique*. Lesser nobles, called *Canahas*, assisted the *Caddi*. In some European and American accounts, the moniker "chief" may have referred to a *Caddi/Cacique* and not a *Xinesi*, as societal structure changed after sustained contact with the Europeans. The positions were all hereditary and traced through the father's line, though a *Xinesi*, *Caddi* or *Canaha* could also be a woman if no sons had been born. Each village or city had at least one *Conna*, or medicine man, who acted as a healer and soothsayer. The position of *Connas* could be inherited or individually discovered through ceremonial vision quests during sweating ceremonies.[13] *Connas* used an extensive knowledge of medicinal plants and herbs. In his seminal work on the Caddo culture, F. Todd Smith pointed out that the entire spiritual world of the Caddos diminished greatly as European trade picked up. While the people still worshipped *Ahahayo* and relied on *Connas*, the role of *Xinesi* seemed to have died out.

Commoners could not rise to the very top (at least, not to any recollection), but distinguished warriors could become *amayxoya*. A successful warrior would bring captives to his village. If the captives were children, tribal families might adopt them and raise them as their own or put them to work as servants. Captive women might be enslaved to families in order to process deer hides, and after European contact, captive adults were sold into slavery to the French. However, after a successful raid, both captive men and women could face torture and death. A captive could be buried in earth up to his neck in order to be beaten or stoned to death by passersby. Henri Joutel wrote of a woman from an enemy tribe of the Hasinais who first had her eye gouged out by the victorious women and then was skewered to death.[14] Other means of torture included ripping out fingernails and hacking limbs. Interestingly, the makeup of the Caddoan chiefdoms, religion and customs very much mirrored Europe's feudal system, right down to a belief in witchcraft, including the burning of witches.[15]

Unlike the Old World, however, run-of-the-mill Caddoan families based their lineage on the mother's clan. Thus, the most important male in a child's family was not necessarily the biological father but the mother's brother. As heads of households, the women built the houses and oversaw the crops; they ruled their families and, by extension, their clans. The oldest or most senior woman in the family held the important task of distributing food, including carrying tributes to ancestor graves. During his visit to the Great Bend region, Henri Joutel paid great deference to the Kadohadacho women; he gave them beads, needles, thread and other items in order to procure provisions. This seemed to be the norm for early Europeans and Anglo Americans who came into contact with the Caddos, as trading "trinkets" gave them a conduit for negotiation.[16] Men farmed alongside their families, but unlike the Plains tribes, farming did not carry with it negative connotations. Men hunted and fished as well. Deer and fish proved their main sources of meat, though occasionally a bison supplemented their diets. Caddoan women used deerskin for their clothing and were considered excellent tanners. The leather was described by French explorers as soft and light as the finest cotton.[17]

Caddoan society was fairly egalitarian, as both men and women worked the fields, harvested, tanned hides and prepared foods for the colder months. One of the main areas of their housing compounds consisted of a wooden deck on which corn was dried and foods prepared, and this was kept meticulously clean.[18] Getting married was a fairly simple and

The Caddos were known far and wide for their pottery. They traded these vessels, Osage Orange (bois d'arc) bows and salt with several other tribes before European invasion. *From the collections of the Arkansas Historical Commission.*

straightforward process, as was getting a divorce, and the Caddos held no stigma against couples who went their separate ways. Joutel wrote that the Kadohadachos "loved their children, but do not have many of them, perhaps because the women do not always stay with the same husband. They leave one another at the least annoyance they have."[19] In later years, Americans who visited the Caddos observed that daughters were sold in marriage, with the bride price usually a horse.[20] These differing descriptions of women's roles mean that either one of the visitors misinterpreted the culture, or the Caddos became less egalitarian after contact with Europeans became more commonplace. The Caddos formed a society that could support a non-working upper caste, an artisan elite and a slave class. This kind of cultural structure assisted them greatly after they made contact with the Spanish and French, as their hierarchies proved similar to those of the Europeans.

The Spanish and French in Southwestern Arkansas

Since the Kadohadachos became the first Caddoan confederacy known to the Europeans, the descriptor "Caddo" was given to all the tribes and clans within the region by the Spanish simply for ease of communication. The name for Texas, however, is famously attributed to the Hasinais, who described the confederacy as friends, or "tejas." The first European to enter Arkansas was Hernando de Soto, who explored much of the American South, from Florida to Texas, in search of gold to populate the coffers of Spain, his near-bankrupt country. De Soto proved to be a cruel, egomaniacal and manipulative adventurer. He viewed the Native Americans he encountered as less than human and "was given to the sport of hunting Indians on horseback."[21] Although the Mississippian chiefdoms he encountered were as intricate a civilization as any he had encountered in Mexico, he and his troops thought nothing of enslaving them, including kidnapping women to become sexual slaves. He brought neck, arm and leg chains with him for that sole purpose, and Native Americans who resisted him, if they had not already succumbed to Old World diseases, could find themselves with disembodied limbs and split noses.

Luckily for the Caddos in southwestern Arkansas, de Soto had already died before his troops, led by Luis de Moscoso Alvarado, visited the Kadohadacho cities along the Red River in 1542. Unfortunately, Moscoso was just as vicious. In a contemporary journal describing de Soto's and Moscoso's expedition, the Spanish troops met numerous scatterings of compounds consisting of houses, farms, storage bins and holding pens on the southwestern banks of the Red River. These settlements are believed to have been located not far from present-day Garland City. Moscoso called this place Naguatex. When the French visited the area a mere century later, Naguatex seemed to have vanished, most likely due to disease. Moscoso's journal explained that the complex was located not far from a salt marsh, at which salt was made, and camp was made "in an open forest of luxuriant and lofty trees."[22] Luis de Moscoso Alvarado and his men camped in Naguatex for almost a month, raiding stores of maize, killing and maiming natives and burning the Naguatex compounds when the Cacique did not do as Moscoso commanded. They also forced natives to work as bearers and guides, who were hanged if they did not do their job correctly.[23]

In 1691, another Spanish expedition into the Great Bend region provided more insight but less chaos. Domingo Teran de los Rios and his men traveled through a large village, occupied by the Nassoni Kadohadachos, that snaked around the Red River west of Naguatex. The expedition brought back with them a detailed map of the village, which included depictions of structures, demarcation of fences and the location of a ceremonial mound. The Teran map, which now resides in an archive in Seville, Spain, has proved invaluable to archaeologists, as it depicts an ancient Caddoan city before disease and warfare took their tolls.

The Spanish were on the hunt for two things—new religious converts and gold—but found neither with the Caddos. Missionaries were not welcomed, as the soldiers they brought with them molested women, destroyed sacred sites and carried disease. An estimated forty thousand Caddos perished in the late seventeenth century due to smallpox, pneumonia, measles and other European ailments.[24] What the Caddos desired were Spanish horses, and long before permanent contact was made with Europeans, the Caddos traded salt and bows for horses with tribes to the west, who already had sustained contact with New Spain.[25] The Spanish never really gained a foothold in the Great Bend region, but they did within the southern confederacies. Among the Hasinais, Nacogdoches, Adaes, Ais and Natchitoches, the Spanish built three missions in the early eighteenth century: San Miguel de los Adaes, Mission Nuestera Senora de los Delores and Mission San Francisco de los Neches. Presidio de los Adaes was built soon after and became the capital of New Spain's Texas province until 1772.[26] Unfortunately for the earnest padres, the Caddos were not interested in becoming catholic; they hoped for trading and military alliance opportunities with the Europeans instead. The Caddos had always traded far and wide. Archaeological evidence at temple mound sites points to extensive trading expeditions that yielded copper procured from the Great Lakes region, greenstone and marble from Appalachia, conch shells from the Caribbean and clay figures from today's Mexico.[27] With the influx of Europeans, the Caddos wanted a firm grip on these new trading opportunities. While the Spanish did not seem to be interested in extending trade, the Caddos welcomed their presidios as defense from the Lipan Apaches and the Osages, nomadic tribes from the Plains and traditional enemies of the Caddos and the Chickasaws, who raided Caddoan settlements to sell captives to English slave markets along the East Coast.[28] Ironically, the missions unintentionally aided French settlements along the Red River as the Caddos and the Spanish monks relied on them for trade in food, materials and, above all, weaponry—the Spanish had a policy of not trading guns with Native Americans, but the French had no such law.[29]

The French proved excellent trading partners to the Caddos, though their beginnings in the Red River Valley were a bit inauspicious. The first major expeditions launched from France were helmed by René-Robert Cavelier,

Sieur de la Salle, a minor nobleman from Rouen on the Seine. During his second discovery voyage of 1670, La Salle laid claim to the Louisiana Territory for the French crown—meaning all lands surrounding waters that flowed into the Mississippi River, which included the Red River Valley. For his last voyage in 1684, La Salle brought four ships and three hundred people to establish a permanent settlement along the southern Mississippi River. Whether accidentally or on purpose, La Salle landed about three hundred miles west of the Mississippi River on Matagorda Bay in today's Texas. The settlers who had not yet died of disease either deserted to live with native tribes, fled to another ship bound to return to France or established a small garrison along Garcitas Creek near Lavaca Bay.[30] Meanwhile, La Salle and his men attempted to find the fort he had established on an earlier voyage along the Illinois River. La Salle never made it back from this journey; he was killed by two or more of his men. Henri Joutel, La Salle's first lieutenant who also, like La Salle, came from Rouen, took over the expedition instead. Leaving the colonists behind, Joutel and his fellow travelers, including Father Anastase Douay and Abbe Jean Cavlier (La Salle's brother), became the first Europeans to extensively record and describe the Red River Valley in southwestern Arkansas.

They traveled first through the Hasinai confederacy, where they witnessed the aftermath of a raid on an unnamed, enemy tribe. The Hasinai warriors had killed and scalped forty warriors and left the battle victorious. What seemed to make the Hasinai successful in the raid was not necessarily their bravery but their weapons: they used French firearms. Deserters from La Salle's expedition had joined the war party, as did Heims, one of La Salle's murderers, and they used their muskets against the enemy. One unfortunate victim was scalped but allowed to live. She was given a bullet and some powder to bring to her vanquished people as a reminder of what power the Hasinais now had. While by the late seventeenth century, the Hasinais already knew about the fierce weapons that the Spanish used, the French actually were willing to share their firepower with them. Thus began an arms race within Native America that made once-powerful tribes dependent on European trade goods.[31]

Though the Hasinais had repeatedly asked him to stay with them, Joutel and his party declined. They desired to keep traveling northeast toward the Mississippi River, though several French troops remained with the tribe. Joutel did promise that, upon his return to France, he would send more trading ships to ensure a steady supply of European trade goods to the Caddos. Joutel well understood the advantages of creating trade partnerships with the native people—after all, his ability to offer goods to the Native Americans he encountered ensured his successful passage.[32]

Following two Indian guides, Joutel and six of his fellow Frenchmen traveled a well-worn Caddoan trading path to the Kadohadachos (in French: Cadohadquis). They crossed forty-one leagues, the equivalent of about 164 miles, over the Sabine and Sulphur Rivers and stopped at one of the oxbow lakes that made up the old channels of the Red River, possibly Roseborough Lake. There, the guides ran ahead to alert the Kadohadacho *caddis* of the impending arrival of the French, and an entire entourage came out to welcome them. Kadohadacho tradition dictated that esteemed visitors must be carried into the village. Henri Joutel, who was of quite impressive size and also carried muskets on him, needed three men to carry him.[33]

Joutel visited the Kadohadachos, who lived in four villages around the Red River in the Great Bend region of southwestern Arkansas, from June 30 to July 2, 1687. "I was quite surprised," he wrote in his journal upon first seeing the Red River, "to see another river, one other than the one we had seen. This one was even more lovely and free of obstruction, as wide as the Seine at Rouen, but its current a little swifter."[34] At the village, the French visitors' faces were washed, and they were greeted by crying women who wanted them to assist in avenging the deaths of their husbands, brothers and sons. The Kadohadachos wanted the French firearms and were willing to put on a big show to gain access to them, as were the other tribes Joutel encountered. It became obvious to Joutel that word of his available trade goods, especially the weapons, had spread throughout the country, and each village he entered put on a bigger display of affection than the last in the hopes of convincing Joutel and his men to stay and help fight their enemies. Once again, Joutel promised that France would be back with more goods. Joutel also noticed that Quapaws were visiting the village at the same time he was. They had come to trade for the Kadohadacho's trademark bows, made of strong and durable bois d'arc wood. The bows were so valuable that the Quapaws traveled "fifty to sixty leagues roundtrip for that purpose."[35] Unfortunately, the influx of French goods a few decades later would make the art of bow manufacturing among the Kadohadachos obsolete.

The French encountered a tragedy among the Kadohadachos when one of their own, Sieur de Marle, drowned in one of the oxbow lakes of the Red River. They buried de Marle in the village and prayed over him with their bibles, which aroused the curiosity of the natives. Over the next few days, Joutel watched as the chief's wife delivered a basket of roasted ears of corn to de Marle's grave as a tribute to his dead friend.[36] Many years later, archaeologists uncovered a grave of a European male whose skeletal ribcage contained two musket balls—it is unknown if de Marle had had a previous injury, or if he actually may have been shot and not drowned.

Joutel and his party left the village to cross the Little River on a raft fashioned out of reeds. Near today's Hope, he met a landscape that "is very beautiful, even more than that of the Cenis [Hasinais], beautiful plains producing fine grass, interspersed with numerous streams lined with lovely trees."[37] He encountered the Cahaymohoa and Quapaw tribes before sailing up the Mississippi River to French holdings in Canada.

Joutel's journals offer a valuable insight into Caddoan life before European invasion. His observations provided a brief glimpse into a vanishing way of life, however, because the arrival of French trade goods signaled a rapid end of the old ways. Within a few decades, the Kadohadachos of the Great Bend region would become very reliant on French trade goods, and they would neglect their own cultural richness in favor of procuring as many furs and hides as needed to gain as many guns as wanted. Trade wars developed between nations. The Chickasaws were especially virulent in their raids on villages to capture people so that they could be sold into slavery, often emptying entire towns or forcing tribes to consolidate for protection. When the Spanish and French first visited, the Kadohadachos numbered about three thousand; during subsequent visits, the census was below five hundred.[38] When the Anglos came to trade with the Kadohadachos, they brought whiskey with them, dooming a people unfamiliar with alcohol. The end of the Caddoan culture began with the arrival of the Europeans, but sadly, the Caddos did not realize this until much, much later.

To the Kadohadachos, the French were their friends. French alliances with the Caddos fostered a creole community in which two very different cultures blended and sometimes flourished.[39] In 1719, a Frenchman named Jean-Baptiste Bernard de la Harpe set up a trading post near a Kadohadachoan/Nasonian city near the Great Bend, which he labeled Nassonite. De la Harpe was commissioned to this post by Jean Baptiste Le Moyne, Sieur de Bienville, governor of the New Orleans district, in order to secure lands that La Salle's expedition had visited for the French crown.[40]

Fort St. Louis de Cadodacho actually consisted only of a small log cabin, a warehouse and a few outbuildings, but it did the trick: the post brought a sustained relationship with the French. De la Harpe received a concession for the lands around the Great Bend of the Red River by de Bienville, who appointed de la Harpe "commandant of the Nassonites, Kadohadachos, Nadocos, and Natchitoches Indians."[41] De la Harpe brought fifty men, two flatboats and three pirogues to the Great Bend. He drew up title to his post between him and the chief in exchange for thirty pistols.[42] Upon his arrival, the Kadohadachos put on a feast of smoked fish and meats for de la Harpe, who explained that he had brought troops and guns to fight with them against the Chickasaws.[13] Though the Spanish were rivals, the French knew they had to engage the Spanish with trade and not warfare, as the Nassonite Post was not supposed to be a fortification but a commercial operation. De Bienville had given de la Harpe a letter to present to Deon Martin de Alcarcon, governor of New Mexico, to indicate peaceful transactions: "Render all services which depend on me to the Spanish nation…I will carry out these orders happily, having no desire than to testify to you on every occasion that no one has the honor of being at your service more than I."[14] On his own, de la Harpe wrote to Father Marsillo, Superior of Texas missions, that though conversion of the heathens was of highest importance, "there is, Reverend Father, a just way of establishing your missions solidly. You know that there are many people who need merchandise."[15] Father Marsillo welcomed trade but warned that the religious should not "become involved in commerce." Marsillo made a political error in his letter: he explained to de la Harpe that the governor of New Mexico had received "several complaints against him…People accuse him of having poorly managed the Indians."[16] This no doubt gave de la Harpe confidence in claiming the land, and trade with the Caddos, for France.

It was through de la Harpe's insistence on claiming the land that boundary disputes over which European nation or American tribe held the territory of southwestern Arkansas began and would not end for over a century. Letters between Martin de Alarconne and Bernard de la Harpe politely but emphatically argued that the lands surrounding the Nassonite Post belonged to their respective kings.[17] "I am compelled to say," d'Alarconne wrote to de la Harpe in 1719, "that your arrival at the Nassonite village surprises me very much. Your governor could not be ignorant that the post you occupy belongs to my Government, and all of the lands west of the Nassonites depend upon New Mexico." De la Harpe countered, "Respecting the post of Nassonite, I can not comprehend by what right you pretend that it forms a part of New Mexico…It was the French who first made alliance with the savage tribes in this region, and it is natural to conclude that a river that flows into the Mississippi and the lands it waters belong to the King, my master."[18]

The Nassonite Post became the center of Kadohadacho life in the Great Bend region. Visitors from other tribes came to trade and smoke the peace pipe. De la Harpe shrewdly offered gifts to the Kadohadachos, who in turn brought more trade goods and pledged allegiance to the French. French men married Kadohadacho women, with the French taking on much of the Caddoan culture. Raids on traditional Caddoan enemies became joint efforts, and New Orleans became a bustling market for the slave trade of captured natives. With the post and relationships established, de la Harpe ventured farther west to meet the tribes along the upper Red River and eventually fostered relationships with the Wichitas, Tonkawas and Keechis.[49]

The Seven Years' War of 1754–63, known as the French and Indian War in American history books, saw the French and Spanish allied against Great Britain, but it did not end well for them; Spain gave up Florida to England, and France gave up the Louisiana Territory to Spain. Suddenly, the Great Bend of the Red River was not in French but Spanish hands. This exchange did not hamper the relationship between French settlers, the Caddos and the creole culture that had developed along the Red River. Spain wanted to exert control, however, and it used a Frenchman to do that. Christophe Athanase Fortunat de Mezieres, a captain in the French army who lived in Natchitoches, struck out to foster peace with, demand allegiance from and attempt to convert the Kadohadachos.[50] In 1770, de Mezieres, Father Miguel Santa Maria y Silva and an entourage of Spanish soldiers came to the Nassonite Post but did not find the Kadohadachos accommodating to the Spanish. The friar wrote of Alexi, a Frenchman who lived in the village and who supplied the Kadohadachos with firearms brought up the Red River from Natchitoches. Alexi apparently held captive several Apache women, whom he "kept…for the infamous traffic of the flesh."[51] This shocked the priest greatly. Father Miguel found the Yatazi village farther down the Red River much more open to his mission. He wrote that the chief was kind and eager to learn more about the religious sacraments that he observed the priest enact, lamenting that the French did not teach his tribe about the European religion but were concerned only with commerce.[52]

In 1773, another attempt at fostering a relationship with the Kadohadachos was made by a Frenchman named Gaignard, who stayed in the Great Bend region for eighty-four days. While Gaignard did not find them hostile, the visit was apparently uneventful, so he made his way up the Red River to seek out the Wichitas.[53] The troubles that de Mezieres, Father Miguel and Gaignard went through to preserve relationships with the Caddos and their neighboring tribes indicate the tight alliances between the French and the Caddos and how much hostility the natives held for the Spanish due to their loyalties to the French.

By the late eighteenth century, another European power had started to seek out trade with the Kadohadachos of southwest Arkansas. The British had begun to trade horses with the Kadohadachos, although they had strong ties with the Chickasaws, the traditional enemy of the Kadohadachos. Because the area west of the Mississippi River was not their territory, however, not much interaction occurred between English and the Kadohadachos until a new nationality appeared: the Americans.

THE AMERICANS COME TO SOUTHWESTERN ARKANSAS

The Spanish wanted religion and gold in the New World; the French wanted trade. The Anglos desired land, and it was through them that the Great Bend region of southwestern Arkansas transformed from a Caddoan empire, set securely as a formidable entity equal to the Spanish and French, to an obstacle to commerce and migration that needed to be vanquished.

In 1798, Louisiana Territory came back under the French flag. In 1803, the territory changed hands once again. James Monroe and Robert Livingston, envoys of the newly formed United States, traveled to France to either purchase New Orleans and its environs or, at least, secure navigation and shipping rights to the ports. The French needed money to quell the Haitian rebellion and wage war against Britain, so they offered a deal: purchase their entire territory of Louisiana—over 800,000 square miles, or all the land that drained into the Missouri and Mississippi Rivers west of the latter—for $15 million, a sum that included the cancellation of French debts. After much bickering with Congress, President Jefferson approved the purchase, and overnight, Arkansas suddenly became American territory.

The Louisiana Purchase doubled the size of the nascent United States, and Jefferson was eager to learn who, and what, composed American land. The president ordered the exploration of this newly acquired territory. Several journeys were ordered, but only two have been extensively recorded for posterity in history books. Everyone with even the most rudimentary knowledge of American history knows about the Lewis and Clark expedition up the Missouri River, and Zebulon Pike's wayward journeys through the Great Plains, into today's Colorado and past the Rio Grande have been well explained, too. What tends to be lesser known is that an equally important expedition was sent to explore the Red River.

Jefferson and his advisors hoped that the Red River reached all the way to Santa Fe. If it did, this would be a boon for trade. Another hope was that the Red River might offer a conduit to the Pacific Ocean, a kind of "southwest passage" that would link the eastern seaboard to the western North American continent. At the very least, exploring the Red River could simply be another outlet for Jefferson's curiosity of the West. The first foray into exploring the territory occurred in 1804, when William Dunbar and George Hunter reconnoitered the Quachita Mountains in Arkansas. A much grander expedition in the manner of Lewis and Clark was set for 1806, with two men at the helm: Peter Custis and Thomas Freeman.

Apparently, this expedition elicited the same excitement for Jefferson as did the Missouri River exploration. He understood that it would be a far more dangerous journey, as the Red River was considered by Spain as a boundary line for New Spain. Since European encroachment had already occurred in the southwest, the United States would be an interloper, not an originator, of contact with the native tribes. The French and the Spanish had already established a firm hold along the river. Thus, one can argue that the Red River expedition held much more political significance than did the Missouri exploration, which at that time was considered virgin land (although French traders were already well established in much of the area). Congress even appropriated twice the amount of money for the journey.

Peter Custis was a twenty-five-year-old naturalist tasked with reporting on the flora and fauna found along the Red River. Thomas Freeman, a surveyor and engineer, would map the river. Richard Sparks led the soldiers who accompanied the crew. The expedition was rounded out by about thirty-seven enlisted men, some of whom were experienced in communicating in sign language with natives. Most of the soldiers were at least a little familiar with the terrain. The group was well outfitted with two flatboats specifically constructed for the trip, pirogues, a large inventory of trade items, scientific and survey equipment, journals, sketching materials, gunpowder and guns, a copy of the current edition of *The Natural Almanac*, maps that were mostly conjecture and proved to be wrong, camping items and food.[54]

The Freeman and Custis expedition began in April 1806. By May, the explorers encountered the first of a series of "Great Rafts" of the Red River north of Natchitoches. The rafts consisted of "the trunks of large trees, lying in all directions, and damming up the river for its whole width, from the bottom, to about three feet higher than the surface of the water. The wood lies so compact that, that [*sic*] large bushes, weeds, and grasses cover the surface of the raft."[55] The raft acted as a dam for the Red River. Water backed up into lakes and bayous, and frequent flooding contributed to the presence of the wide flood plains, or flat prairies, in southwestern Arkansas. The swamps proved terrible to navigate, as they "hid" the actual riverbed, and much time was wasted backing away from dead ends. Upon entering the open waters of the Red River north of the raft, Custis speculated that "were the Rafts removed so as to admit of navigation this country in very short time would become the Paradise of America."[56] His advice was heeded a few decades later by the U.S. government, which ordered the clearing of the raft.

In June and July, the party met a Coushatta village and camped there for a while. The Coushattas were an Alabama tribe that relocated to the

Louisiana Territory in the late eighteenth century, possibly due to attacks by the Chickasaws. Here, the expedition was greeted by the great leader of the Kadohadachos, Dehahuit. Dehahuit would figure prominently in later negotiations with the Caddo confederacy and the Americans. The chief wished them well and hinted that he would be most pleased if the expedition would kill any Osages they met.[57] Waging war, of course, was not the purpose of the expedition. What is notable is that Freeman and Custis did not encounter a great number of Kadohadachos; in fact, the population may have been only in the low hundreds. While continuous warfare with other tribes may have played a small role, the main culprit of the diminished population was probably disease, possibly cholera and smallpox. The reduced size of the Kadohadachos did not dampen their open spirit, however. Dehahuit promised Custis and Freeman two guides and interpreters, Cut Finger and Grand Ozages, who would accompany them for the rest of their journey.[58]

As the expedition proceeded farther upriver, they observed that the Red River in Arkansas "cannot be exceeded either in fertility or beauty, by any part of America, or perhaps of the world."[59] Custis was especially awed by the diversity of the trees, specifically the large red cedar groves that grew around the river.[60] The two Caddoan guides, Cut Finger and Grand Ozages, led the party to the Medicine Mount, a sacred site near today's Lewisville where, according to tradition, the Caddoan people originated.[61] Freeman wrote that once, according to Cut Finger and Grand Ozages, a large Caddoan village was located near the mountain, but the expedition could not find a trace of it when they passed through. Considering that Medicine Mount is near Spirit Lake, it is possible that the party was near the abandoned location of Naguatex.

But trouble lay on the horizon. Spanish troops had entered the Coushatta village where Dehahuit resided, cut down the American flag and warned that the explorers may be killed or jailed. Dehahuit sent men to alert the expedition that over two hundred Spanish soldiers were monitoring their moves. To thwart the Spanish, Custis and Freeman hid their journals and instruments near Hemphill Lake in today's Little River County, close to where the Nassonite Post founded by Benard de la Harpe once stood.[62] They continued to travel along the river until they came upon the Spanish encampment at a high, rocky bluff on the south side of the river. Here, Spanish commander Captain Francisco Viana and his soldiers charged the Red River expedition.[63] A brief but nonviolent standoff ensued, as both Viana and Sparks, the American military leader of the expedition, knew that firing on sovereign nations may invoke war. Viana demanded that the Americans not continue their mission, since boundary lines remained unclear and they were intruding on territory claimed by Spain. Freeman asked Viana to put this in writing, which he did. The Americans retreated downriver the following day.[64]

While the Red River expedition of 1806 proved ultimately unsuccessful, it did provide quite a bit of insight into the Red River Valley that America wanted to claim. Peter Custis brought back with him an amazing catalogue of native flora and fauna, including documentations of parakeets, falcons, bears, herbs, trees, grasses and more. The journey also established how fertile the valley was, who inhabited it, what the political climate would be and how much ire the Americans would draw when they tried to settle. All of this information would prove invaluable to American settlement efforts.

It wasn't until 1856 that the Red River's whole length was documented. Captain Randolph B. Marcy, Brevet George McClellan, dragoons and Indian guides followed the river from just north of Sherman, Texas, to its origin. Along the way, they met with Wichitas, Comanches and Kiowas; discovered a petrified forest; marveled at a prairie dog city with a population of close to 20 million critters; and waxed poetic about the dramatic Palo Duro Canyon, which rose from the prairie with blood-red rock formations, being second in size only to the Grand Canyon. Unlike Custis and Freeman, Marcy returned to Washington, D.C., a conquering hero.[65]

Southwestern Arkansas—or Northeastern Mexico?

To make the new territory easier to govern, Congress divided it into two parts: the Louisiana Territory, which encompassed the boundaries of today's state of Louisiana, and the Missouri Territory, which included the rest of the Louisiana Purchase. This division did not last long, however. By 1812, Louisiana Territory was admitted to the Union as a state. Other territories would be carved out of the Missouri Territory as soon as boundary lines and population minimums were established. Thus, Congress formed the territory of Arkansas in 1819. Until 1828, the territory included most of today's Oklahoma.

Joseph Hardin, speaker of the House in 1820, wrote enthusiastically about the destiny of Arkansas Territory to President James Monroe, saying,

"[It] is situated in the southwestern extreme of the American Republic. It borders Mexico and fills the space which intervenes between Missouri and Louisiana; and we [Hardin and Governor Miller] believe when populated it will form a barrier to the dominions of Spain and will act in the protection of the great emporium of the west."[66]

Pioneers wanted to fulfill Hardin's prediction by becoming the vanguards of manifest destiny. To get to southwestern Arkansas, potential settlers could take two routes. One involved boating from the Mississippi to the Red River, struggling through the Great Raft and then entering into Arkansas from the south. Or the nascent farmers could walk southwest from Memphis over poorly maintained toll roads and ancient Indian footpaths. This patchwork of byways formed the Southwest Trail, which would later become a very prominent emigrant and military road. So many people began flooding into the Red River country that by 1819, the territorial government established Hempstead County, named after Edward Hempstead, a representative from the Missouri Territory. The county's governance extended into today's Lafayette, Nevada, Pike, Howard and Sevier Counties. The earliest settlement in the county was Mound Prairie, named for the impressive Caddoan ceremonial mounds located in its vicinity. The location of the Hempstead Courthouse, originally at Marlbrook near today's Blevins, was moved to the burgeoning settlement of Washington in 1825. About twenty miles distant from the Red River and situated along the Southwest Trail, Washington quickly grew into one of Arkansas' most prominent towns.

By 1820, census records showed that Hempstead County had 2,248 white inhabitants.[67] Enough people had moved into the Great Bend region to warrant the creation of Miller County, named to honor the first territorial governor of Arkansas, James Miller. The original Miller County was huge. Formed from parts of Hempstead County, it encompassed today's Miller and Little River Counties in Arkansas; McCurtain, Choctaw, Bryan, Pushmataha and Atoka Counties in today's Oklahoma; and the future Texas counties of Fannin, Lamar, Red River, Bowie, Cass, Morris, Titus, Franklin, Hopkins and Delta. Due to boundary disputes and questions about legal organization, Miller County never had an official county seat; official business was conducted at houses in the two prominent settlements that bordered the river, Pecan Point and Jonesboro. In 1827, Lafayette County was organized out of Hempstead County. Lafayette's courthouse sat along the Red River north of Walnut Hill, a prosperous plantation owned by James Sevier Conway, the first governor of the state of Arkansas. The location of the courthouse was soon moved to La Grange, across the river from the Long Prairie settlements.[68]

Harper's Weekly depicted a pioneer camp in Arkansas as a rough-and-tumble place. *Courtesy Library of Congress.*

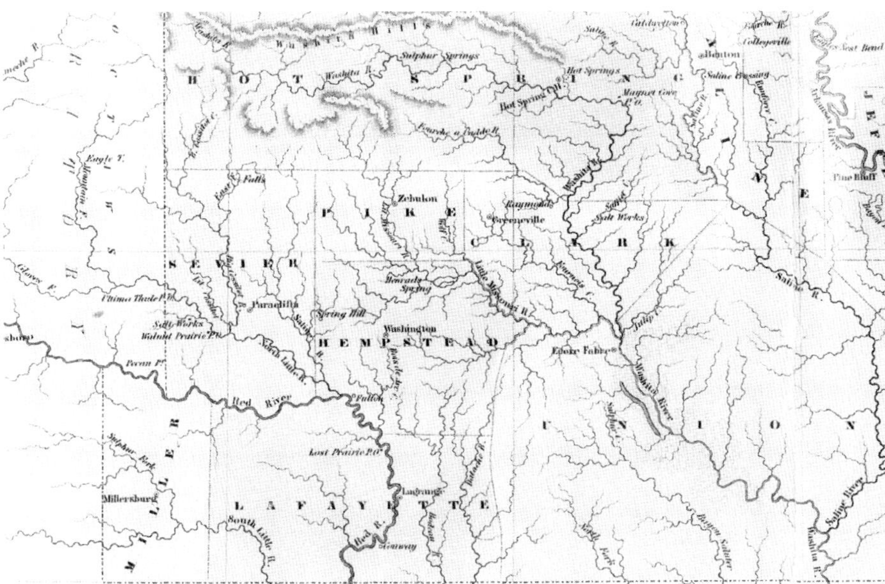

A map from the 1830s shows the locations of post offices and settlements in southwestern Arkansas. By this time, Miller County had been reduced—it used to encompass Pecan Point and Jonesboro to the west. *From the collections of the Arkansas Historical Commission.*

Native American tribes still inhabited their ancestral lands, however, and though they may have numbered only in the high hundreds at this time, Americans nonetheless considered them a barrier to progress. From 1819 to 1821, the Sulphur River Indian Factory was established at the confluence of the Red and Sulphur Rivers in southern Miller County. The agency, a trading post set up by the Office of Indian Trade, was supposed to monitor interactions between the whites and the natives, assist Indians in assimilating to white ways, act as a way station for information and trade and stave off attacks and depredations. Further, the agency was charged with handling whatever compensation the tribes received for the takeover of their lands. Dehahuit, the Caddo chief who at first welcomed the Americans to his country, was not interested in receiving money. Alarmed by the influx of Americans, he attempted to claim all land above the Red River raft for his people, but the American response was simply to suggest that the Caddos elect a new chief.[69] The disinterest in the Caddo chief demonstrated the general contempt and dismissal of Native Americans by the new settlers, except when tribes tried to assert their authority—then Americans immediately sought relief through official means. For example, Nathaniel Robbins and Lewis Dayton of Pecan Point complained to Jose Antonio Saucedo, police chief of the Department of Texas for Mexico, that although settlers had to pay taxes to the United States, it did not provide protection from Indian raids.[70] Early settlers who complained of raids by Shawnees and Osages received permission from both Mexico and Miller County to form provisional governments and/or militias.[71]

Perceived trouble with Native Americans, whether real or exaggerated, was one of many catalysts of animosity between the United States and Mexico regarding the official boundary of each country. Should not the Red River of southwestern Arkansas and west thereof serve as the border between the nations, or did the entire Red River watershed belong to the United States? A few settlers played a game of chance and established themselves south of the Red River. Pecan Point, sometimes called Pecan Plantation, lies in today's Red River County, Texas. Nothing more than a small settlement and never having a post office, Pecan Point lay on a prominent loop of land that jutted into the Red River from the southern shore. Pecan Point was only a few miles upstream from Spanish Bluff, where the confrontation between Vania and the Freeman/Custis expedition took place. By 1816, Henry Jones set up a trading post west of Pecan Point on the south shore of the river, which locals named Jonesboro. The American settlers insisted that they had landed in Arkansas Territory, but this was not really clear, of course. Traditional history tends to view the settlers as being merely confused by the boundaries. Along the Great Bend, their misperception is understandable, as the river changes its direction from flowing east to flowing south. However, the Red River at Pecan Point and Jonesboro clearly marks the division between land to the north and land to the south. Therefore, one can surmise that the motivations of the settlers might have been to claim the land south of the Red River for the United States—an act of filibustering. This may have come with a sense of urgency, too, when Mexico outlawed slavery in 1826, and many settlers relied on slavery to support their economy.[72]

Initially, many Pecan Point settlers agreed on where their loyalties should lie. In an 1821 letter to the governor of Spanish Texas, Jonesboro resident William Rabb emphatically stated, "It is the opinion of the most intelligent men in this section that we are within the limits of the Province of Texas."[73] According to historian Rex Strickland, who discovered the letter, Rabb may have simply been venting about the levying of taxes on his land and would have declared loyalty to the United States had New Spain begun collecting taxes, too. Pecan Point settlers hedged their bets with New Spain, then with Mexico when it won its independence from Spain in 1824. "A number of inhabitants on the south side of the river consider themselves as Spanish subjects," wrote Richard Walsh, lieutenant of the Seventh Infantry, to Matthew Arbuckle, commandant at Cantonment Gibson, in 1823, "and consider themselves no longer subject to the laws of the United States."[74] According to historian Lonnie J. White, one of the main reasons Pecan Point settlers insisted on being subject to New Spain was to ensure that they received title to their lands.[75] Another look at the overall history of the region tends to suggest that allegiance to either country depended on that government's support of the settlers' hostility toward Native Americans. For example, Pecan Point settlers began to assert their ties to New Spain/Mexico after the United States allotted the Choctaws land in western Miller County in 1825 but would become "American" again when the Mexican government gave the Shawnees land grants to settle nearby.

The "confusion" as to which country governed Miller County, Arkansas Territory, lasted several years. The boundary between the countries was supposedly settled in 1819 with a treaty signed by John Quincy Adams, then secretary of state under President James Monroe, and Louis de Onis, Spanish minister to the United States. The treaty stipulated that, in exchange for east and west Florida, the United States would give up claims to Texas. Further, the boundary between New Spain, west of the Mississippi, would "begin on the Gulf of Mexico, at the mouth of the

River Sabine in the Sea, continuing North, along the Western Bank of that River, to the 32d degree of Latitude, thence by a Line due North to the degree of Latitude, where it strikes the Rio Roxo of Natchitoches, or Red River, then following the course of the Rio-Roxo Westward to the degree of Longitude, 100 West from London and 23 from Washington, then crossing the said Red-River."[76] In other words, the Red River north of Natchitoches and then all the way west until the 100th Meridian, was meant to serve as the border. Thus, most of Miller County, Arkansas Territory, was supposed to be under Spanish dominion. The treaty was upheld by the new government of Mexico after the Mexican Revolution of 1824. In 1830, Mexico surveyed their lands according to the treaty and laid claim to most of Miller County. Because of the claims, Miller County residents held circuit court hearings only sporadically and usually inside the house of one of its leading citizens, having foregone the need to erect a county seat until the dispute was settled.[77] American governments on the national and local levels were not ready to cede to the survey, however.

Continuing to insist that the boundaries were not officially established, American politicians like John Pope (Arkansas territorial governor, 1829–35) and William Fulton (secretary for Governor Pope and, later, Arkansas territorial governor, 1835–36) wrote about their apprehensions over the disputed border to Secretary of State Martin van Buren. They were especially concerned about James Bowie and Benjamin Milam, two Americans who briefly stayed in the Great Bend region before heading off to Texas and into its mythology. In 1829, James Bowie and an accomplice, Ashley Crittenden, attempted to profit from the boundary confusion by claiming and selling land grants using fictitious papers that were apparently manufactured in Louisiana. The Spanish used in the legal writings was riddled with errors, garnering much suspicion.[78] Benjamin Milam, on the other hand, had a legitimate enterprise. Armed with a genuine land grant from Mexico, he entered Miller County in 1830 and opened a land office in order to establish a Mexican colony on the Red River. Milam explained to Americans who had already settled on the land—like those who lived at Pecan Point, Jonesboro and Lost Prairie—that they could stay if they signed loyalty oaths to Mexico, which many of the inhabitants were willing to do. Fearing an international incident, William Fulton, under Martin van Buren's direction, asked Mexico to halt Milam's agenda, assuring the nation that "every effort will be made on our part" to halt immigration until the boundaries could be settled. Mexico agreed, with Fulton praising the "liberal spirit manifested by

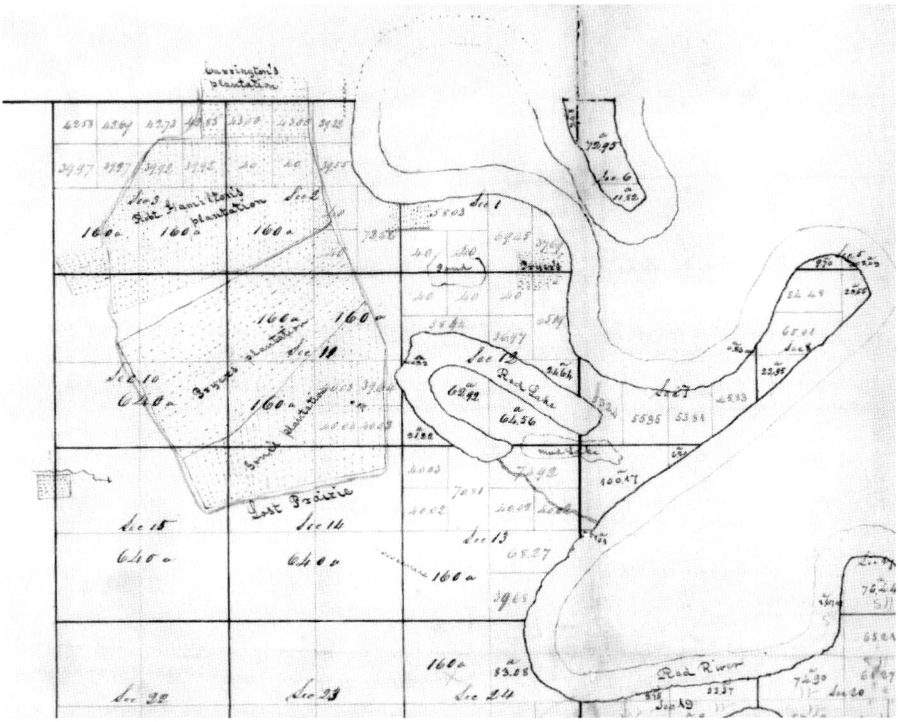

Lost Prairie is depicted on this early Lafayette County plat. The area west of the Red River was claimed by Mexico. Robert Hamilton, who owned plantations at Lost Prairie and Pecan Point, was one of the signers of the Texas Declaration of Independence. *From the collections of the Arkansas Historical Commission.*

the Mexican government."[79] Of course, the flood of American migrants could not be stemmed. Mexico ceded the land, instead, "as an act of prudence and for the good of harmony," wrote General Jose Teran of Mexico in 1831.[80] Other efforts by the Mexican government to establish its dominion over lands south of the Red River included giving land grants in Pecan Point to the Shawnees, who entered the area with official documentation in 1831. Immediately, the white settlers accused the Shawnees of raiding houses and corn cribs, destroying pecan trees and killing hogs. The whites raised a militia, and though the Shawnees were ready to fight, they eventually agreed to leave the area.[81]

Considering that the whites did not arm themselves against Benjamin Milam's claims but did so immediately against the Indians, this demonstrated their mounting hatred of Native Americans. For Texans—whether they were hedging their bets as Mexican or American citizens or joining the Texas

Revolution a decade later—this hatred tinged every aspect of their dealings with indigenous people.

The question over national sovereignty along the Red River would be answered through a series of events. The disputed western half of Miller County became Indian Territory by 1830. By 1838, Arkansas (by then a state) dissolved Miller County completely in acknowledgement of the claims laid by the Republic of Texas. Lafayette County absorbed the remaining Arkansas portion of Miller County.

THE CHOCTAWS AND CHICKASAWS IN SOUTHWESTERN ARKANSAS

The dispute over where the United States ended and Mexico began was not the only concern over which entity governed which side of Miller County. Historian Patricia Nelson Limerick once wrote that the American West embodied a crossroads of diversity, and southwestern Arkansas served as a prime example.

After many failed attempts by the whites to coerce the Choctaws into giving up their lands, the Choctaws signed their first removal treaty in 1820. The Treaty of Doak's Stand between the Choctaws and the United States granted the tribe lands in Arkansas Territory in exchange for their ancestral lands in Mississippi. The only people happy with this land exchange were the southern planters who lusted after the potential cotton kingdoms in the Mississippi River basin that the Choctaws would leave behind; the Choctaws and the residents of Miller County both found the treaty reprehensible. The Choctaws were not impressed with the quality of the land in Arkansas Territory, being used to more watery soils, abundant lakes and denser forests. They had to give up their homes, farms and villages to move to a foreign land, all because American Indian policy rested on the belief that tribes should not be independent but instead subservient to the United States in order to ward off extinction. By this point in history, however, many Choctaws had already given up their traditional ways—in religion, dress and customs—to take on the "white man's ways." Some individual Choctaws even owned plantations and slaves. Still, tribal chiefs felt coerced to sign the treaty by Andrew Jackson, who acted as the U.S. agent. Due to their reluctance over this treaty, Choctaw migration to Arkansas Territory would take over a decade to complete and necessitated another treaty in 1830. The United

States wanted removal to occur much quicker, however, and immediately began the preparations for the ejection of the Choctaws.

Initially, the *Arkansas Gazette* reported that all of Miller County would be swallowed by the Choctaw land exchange, but that turned out to be false. Due to a supposedly faulty survey done by William Rector in 1819, the boundaries could not be completely determined and remained in question until a new 1825 survey by William Clark rectified them.[82] Nonetheless, panic ensued among the settlers of Miller County. One anonymous resident declared in a letter to the editor of the *Arkansas Gazette* that "this very tract of country contains more than three thousand hardy, industrious inhabitants" who will have "to make room for ruthless savages." The letter writer warned that Miller County whites may move to Texas.[83] In response to the Treaty of Doak's Stand, Arkansas territorial governor James Miller (1819–24) advised that the removal of the whites who had already settled Miller County would bankrupt them and lamented that the Choctaws were to receive lands that held potential riches of coal, lead, iron ore, salt and more.[84] The anxiety of the Americans at Pecan Point and Jonesboro who found themselves in the middle of this land changeover may have fueled their desire to be claimed as Mexican, not American, citizens, so as to circumvent the entire question of their land claims. North of the Red River, however, the boundary was certain; thus, by 1823, almost 375 families, or over 2,500 settlers, were forced off the land.[85] Claiborne Wright, the sheriff of Miller County, conducted an official accounting of the loss to the settlers. He estimated that with over six thousand acres of cultivated land, which included five hundred acres of cotton, a cotton gin and two corn gristmills, the losses would be staggering.[86] One of the settlers who was forced off his land was James Black, who lost his house and mill. He moved to Washington, where he opened a blacksmith shop, in which he fashioned the famous Bowie knife.[87]

The whites petitioned the U.S. government in the hopes of halting their removal. One 1825 petition explained that since Miller County had been carved out of Hempstead County, for which the U.S. government had fairly compensated the Quapaw tribe, the Choctaw land exchange should not be legal. The petition, which was signed by Bailey Inglish, Jesse Cheek, Claiborne Wright and other Miller County settlers, had no bearing on the ultimate outcome, possibly because the land had been set aside for preparation of Native American removal already by 1818. But the federal government did decide to allow the whites to wait until their crops were gathered before they moved.[88]

To facilitate the migration of the Choctaws, the army erected Cantonment Towson, a few miles north of the Red River above Jonesboro, in 1824. The

A Choctaw couple, complete with elaborate tattoos, is depicted in an engraving by Bernard Romans for *A Concise Natural History of East and West Florida* (1775). *Courtesy Library of Congress.*

idea for the fort, which was proposed by John Fowler, the overseer of the Sulphur River Indian Factory, was that it would protect surveyors, Choctaws and indigenous Native Americans from the mounting hostility along this uneasy border.[39] Anger stayed in check until 1825, when a new survey by William Clark placed the Choctaw Nation in western Miller County. The area encompassed today's McCurtain, Pushmataha, Choctaw, Atoka and Bryan Counties in Oklahoma. To solidify the established borders for the Choctaw Nation, Miller County was retracted into southwestern Arkansas territory and today's northeastern Texas, and the federal government declared the Choctaw portion as part of the Indian Territory.

The white settlers, with anger and resentment boiling over, lashed out against the fort. Calls for its closure came at frequent intervals, and Alex Cummings, the fort commander, complained to his superiors of the unruly whites who molested the Native Americans—Choctaws, Caddos, Osages and others—who asserted their claims to the land. Requesting more troops, he wrote in 1827, "We are in the neighborhood of a large Indian population who are under no controul [*sic*]...The whites, most of who are no better than the savages, are constantly coming in collision with them, and numerous complaints are made of horses being stolen, or property plundered from one or the other of them…I will do the Indians the justice to say, that so far as I can learn, they are more sinn'd against than sinning."[90] In another letter, Cummings rightly pointed out that much of Miller County lay on the principal hunting grounds of the Osages, Caddos and Pawnees and that the tribes used the Red River bottoms to plant corn.[91] Cummings, therefore, seemed to feel no allegiance to the white settlers and refused to aid them when help for yet another perceived injustice was requested. One particular thorn in Cummings's side was Jesse Cheek, a white settler from Pecan Point whom he accused of selling liquor to the fort's soldiers. The *Arkansas Gazette* reported in 1825 that Cheek had attempted to murder Cummings.[92] Cheek and other whites petitioned Arkansas territorial attorney general Roane to indict Cummings on charges of misconduct stemming from a raid by soldiers on settlers at Pecan Point. Roane, who appeared not to like Cummings, the fort or the removal, did not heed their request but expressed sympathy for the American settlers.[93] In 1829, a few "desperate villains, in a frolic, set fire to the barracks at Cantonment Towson, and burnt them to the ground."[94] The fort was rebuilt and remained occupied into the 1840s, when it served soldiers bound for the battlefields of the Mexican-American War. Closed for good in the 1850s, it became a Confederate garrison in the Civil War. After 1865, locals used the fort's building materials to erect their own abodes, and today, the fort consists of ruins inside a state park.

After the election of Andrew Jackson in 1828, the reluctant Choctaws signed the Treaty of Dancing Rabbit Creek in 1830, which called for removal with military accompaniment and under a three-year deadline. The Choctaw chiefs Mushlatubee and Nitakechi, who had signed the earlier treaty, protested that many of the men who signed the new treaty did not represent the entire Choctaw tribe. Using Chief Pushmataha's reasoning, they believed that since several of the signers had white blood, they were therefore more likely to acquiesce to land cessions. It turned out to be true: many of the signers of the Treaty of Dancing Rabbit Creek may have not had the best interests of the tribe at stake, because in return for their signatures, they received large, individual tracts of land. However, doubts did not seem to matter to the new federal administration, the sole goal of which became to disband the nation's sovereignty and remove the tribe west. The removal requirements included the Chickasaw nation. The Chickasaws, who had not come to terms with the U.S. government over the sale and exchange of their traditional homelands, instead decided to lease the western portion of the new Choctaw lands until an agreeable settlement for their properties in Mississippi could be reached.[95]

The grave of Choctaw chief Pushmataha in Washington, D.C. Chief Pushmataha reluctantly signed the treaties that eventually ceded the Choctaw homelands in Mississippi in exchange for land in Indian Territory. *Courtesy Library of Congress.*

Military leaders told the citizens of Hempstead and Sevier Counties to begin preparations, and notices in the *Arkansas Gazette* by the federal government asked for bids to supply provisions for the thousands of people who would eventually cross Hempstead County to their new homeland. Many Hempstead County residents added more livestock and raised more corn, built warehouses and supply depots, dug wells and constructed bridges (many done hastily and shoddily) to be ready for the marchers.[96]

The forced migration for the Choctaws began in 1831, with the largest influx in 1832 and 1833; for the Chickasaws, the largest numbers were reported in 1838.[97] The route of this southern "Trail of Tears" was long and circuitous due to bad roads, few river crossings, shortsighted planning and unscrupulous men. The plan was to board boats at Vicksburg or Memphis, steam up or down the Mississippi River to the Arkansas River and then disembark at Little Rock. From there, the migrants were supposed to walk to Washington in Hempstead County and then turn west to follow the Fort Towson road, which had been cut and prepared by troops from the fort. This journey was supposed to take only two or three months, but due to food shortages, low rations, cholera outbreaks, bad weather and sabotage, the Choctaws endured horrific hardships. Early arrivals soon discovered that preparations, especially food storage, were inadequate. George S. Gaines, a white dry goods store owner from Mississippi who was trusted by the Choctaws, closed his store in the old Choctaw lands to move out west with the tribe. Choctaw elders asked him to oversee the move and the allotment of supplies, which the tribe had to buy and manage with the monies it received as part of the treaty.

Captain Jacob Brown, who accompanied the Choctaws, recounted impassable roads, high water and the fact that, due to delays, the Choctaws were not prepared for the oncoming brutal winter of 1831–32. With only summer clothing—and many of the children not wearing much clothing at all—the extreme cold, little availability of blankets and six inches of snow left many Choctaws dead or incapacitated. Brown did not have good things to say about some inhabitants of Hempstead County, who "practiced bare-faced extortions to the Indians and the government...[the Choctaws were] obliged to purchase food from heartless conspirators at exorbitant prices."[98] He mentioned that cattle purchased from traders ended up being wild and bolted, and bridges and ferries, built specifically to handle the influx of people, "were mysteriously destroyed" in order to glean even more money for their repair or replacement.[99] However, many good citizens were appalled by the scenes they witnessed of starving, ill-clad people being forced to relocate to an unknown land and tried to help as best they could. One woman recalled her grandfather offering his turnip garden to anyone in need, and the supply depots at Washington, Jonesboro and Fort Towson were manned by mostly honest men, like Josiah S. Doaks (after whom the first Choctaw town in Indian Territory, Doaksville, was named).

The Chickasaws fared slightly better than the Choctaws on their resettlement. Having adapted successfully to the southern economy, many members of the Chickasaw nation owned plantations and slaves. Several sold their properties in Alabama and Mississippi and came by wagon or paddle-wheeler to their new homes in Indian Territory, paying for the move out of their own funds. However, the *Arkansas Gazette* reported a smallpox outbreak in a group of migrants in September 1838, and the Chickasaws discovered that their new lands were too close for comfort to Kiowa and Comanche territories. The Chickasaws also did not have their own government, having been removed alongside the Choctaws under their treaty provisions. The Chickasaws reestablished their sovereignty and became a nation separate from the Choctaws in 1856.

The plights of the Choctaws and Chickasaws were mirrored in the removals of the Cherokees, Seminoles and Creeks into Indian Territory. John Sibley, Indian agent at Natchitoches, summed up the apprehension about the forced land sales and exchanges that many westerners felt in this early period of expansion: "I have always deprecated the policy of sending so many Indians back to this defenseless frontier; it seems to me, if our government wanted us destroyed, the same policy would be pursued."[100]

People in Slavery and Free People of Color in Southwestern Arkansas

The Anglos who ventured to southwestern Arkansas were mostly of southern stock and brought their southern ways with them, including a plantation system based on slavery. Early white settlers may have brought none or only one or two enslaved people with them, as they were generally not very wealthy. Often, slaves of the early settlers worked alongside the white men in building houses and establishing farms.

People who owned prosperous plantations in more established states speculated on Arkansas land to grow upland cotton, which, thanks to the cotton gin, could be processed by slaves more efficiently. Working and living conditions on these absentee-owned plantations could be brutal. The threat of going to a cotton plantation "out west"—meaning Arkansas, Texas or Louisiana—was used to keep enslaved people in line. A system of perpetual slavery based on skin color also led to classifications of enslaved people. In sale records and runaway notices, enslaved people were classified by their skin color as either yellow, dark, copper, mulatto, black bright mulatto or light.[101]

When carving the Missouri Territory out of the Louisiana Purchase, questions persisted as to whether Congress would allow the newly acquired land to permit slavery. The Missouri Compromise of 1820 established that while Missouri could enter the Union as a slave state, any other territory requesting to become a state that sat above the thirty-sixth parallel could not allow slavery in its constitution. Territories that formed below the line could choose to enter the Union as slave or free states. Arkansas Territory, of course,

A ferry crosses the Red River during a freshet—high water—in this depiction created for *Harper's Weekly*. Horses apparently had to swim behind the flotilla. The ferry is pulled across the river to keep it from veering off course. *Courtesy Library of Congress.*

sat below the thirty-sixth parallel. That fact, however, did not automatically create a unified block in allowing slavery. Many of the early politicians for the territory were from free states, and abolitionists in Congress, like John W. Taylor of New York, agitated to create a slave-free territory.[102] The end result followed the custom of the South, however, and Arkansas Territory allowed slavery.

The early southwestern counties of Hempstead, Miller and Lafayette implemented slave codes, which included how many lashes an enslaved person was supposed to receive as penance for infractions, what could be done with children born into slavery and whether marriage was permitted. Counties also regulated the movements of "free persons of color."[103] In Hempstead County, for example, a free person of color had to receive a "certificate of character," which included references and physical descriptions. He or she needed official documentation to travel and had to register with the county if he or she desired to settle there.[104] By 1843, Arkansas forbade the emigration of any free people of color, and a law passed in 1859 stipulated that free people of color must either leave the state or become enslaved. One such victim was Jake Madden of Hempstead County, a free black man who also owned slaves. He left Arkansas and settled in California, where he became wealthy.[105]

Like other southern states, Arkansas passed a comprehensive slave code when it was admitted to the Union, which mirrored the earlier ones implemented by the counties. The emphasis was on behavior control: enslaved people could not "sell, barter, or deliver, to any other slave any vinous or spirituous liquors"; could not possess a firearm; could not travel; and could not assemble or speak seditiously. Whites, mulattos or free blacks faced "any number of stripes not exceeding thirty" if they were caught gambling, drinking, harboring or entertaining enslaved people. The importation of a slave who had committed a felonious crime or who had a history of agitation was prohibited. The final control of an enslaved person rested with his or her "master," which, in essence, required a legal system based on the wills and whims of white men. The treatment of enslaved women was not broached at all.[106]

Since southern wealth rested on land and slaves, enslaved people were used as payments for debts. Hempstead County deed records indicate that whole families could be disbanded to settle lawsuits. A sheriff's sale in 1845 offered "husband Zenas, wife Eliza, three young children Moses, James and David" for sale to pay the debts of George Conway to Benjamin C. Brittin.[107] Sometimes, slaves were not sold but exchanged for this purpose. Slaves were quite expensive—those who could perform skilled labor, such as blacksmithing or horseshoeing, could be "priced" over $1,500—and many purchasers financed through mortgages. Joshua Morrison of Lafayette County bought twenty-six slaves from dealers in Mississippi in 1834 for $30,000, with 10 percent interest. In an 1842 mortgage agreement in Hempstead County, "the labor of Lynda, a slave woman, will pay interest on the loan of $190." Enslaved people could also be presented as gifts to relatives. In Lafayette County, John Bradley gave his mother a "gift of Haina, female, 30" in 1822, and Nicholas Trammel deeded an enslaved woman named Mary and her child to his daughter Nancy Baker in 1841. Often, the gifts to daughters came with stipulations that sons-in-law not be allowed to mortgage or sell their wives' slaves.[108]

Many Americans described the practice of human slavery as "the peculiar institution," and deed records can attest to the strangeness of the practice. It was brutal on the oppressed and brutalized the oppressor, but it could also, on some occasions, overcome the inhumanity—after all, humans, regardless of their skin color, cannot help but form bonds, leading some owners to emancipate their slaves. Colleen Grayham of Lafayette County emancipated Robert in 1829 "for and in consideration of the honest, integrity, and meritorious services which have been rendered." Through careful reading of deed records, one can surmise that slave owners may have emancipated the children they had conceived with enslaved women. Joseph Glass emancipated William, "the son of a negro woman called Eliza, born February 9, 1842 and supposed to be half-white" in 1844. John C. Gowder manumitted a woman named Jane, who was thirty, and her seven children "from motives of benevolence and humanity" in 1855. Slave owners, regardless of their belief that they enjoyed a good relationship with their slaves, nonetheless understood the adversarial nature of enslavement. John Holeman of Hempstead County stipulated that he would free a woman named Rose upon his death but wrote that emancipation would occur only if Rose continued to "conduct herself well and treat me kindly."[109] One will by a man named William Reed stipulated that Salmon Ruggles, who received the enslaved James as an inheritance, must emancipate James by the age of twenty-six after teaching him how to read.[110]

Enslaved people often took their fates in their own hands, whether it was through passive resistance or by running away. It may have been especially enticing for slaves to try to escape to Texas while it was still under Mexican rule, as Mexico prohibited slavery in 1826. Others may have tried to escape into Indian Territory. Seeking to recapture runaway slaves was not an uncommon occurrence in the southwest. Robert Hamilton, one of the signers of the Texas declaration of independence who owned two plantations in the Great Bend region—one in Pecan Point, Miller County, the other on Lost Prairie in Lafayette County—placed an advertisement describing four runaway or stolen slaves in the *Arkansas Gazette* in 1840.[111] One particularly sad story involved an entire family of runaway slaves. Charles; his wife, Penny; and their two children, Mary and Harriet, apparently attempted to flee Louisiana. They were discovered in Lafayette County in January 1832 and were arrested and jailed in La Grange.[112] Enslaved people who were discovered traveling without proper paperwork or who claimed to have been kidnapped to be sold at New Orleans slave markets were imprisoned until someone claimed responsibility for them and paid a fine.

Being an enslaved person meant a life consigned to hard labor. As larger plantations grew from the southwestern Arkansas soil, so did the number of slaves, who were forced to dedicate their lives to picking cotton or to serve in the households of their owners. During harvest, fieldwork took place six days a week, from sun up to sun down. Hogs, chickens, cows and vegetable gardens were tended to before and after the fieldwork, making for exhausting and endless days. Children were bought as playmates or kept the masters and mistresses cool as they ate or slept by waving large fans. Women worked in the fields, as wet nurses or as servants. Enslaved women faced the additional threat of being raped and could face whippings if they resisted sexual advances.[113] The general superintendent of the Freedmen's Bureau for the State of Arkansas commented on the scars women bore from the lashes they received to force them into sexual subservience.[114] Both men and women could be "allotted," which meant they could be rented or sold with a mortgage attached. "Times don't change," said Sarah Graves, a former slave, "just the merchandise."[115]

Advertisements of "Negroes for Sale" appeared in the *Arkansas Gazette* frequently, along with the offer of other agricultural products for purchase. One such advertisement read, "Will be sold, at public auction, at Spring Hill, in the county of Hempstead, on a credit of twelve months, on Friday, the 28th day of this present month, fifteen young and valuable slaves, consisting of nine superior men and boys, between twelve and twenty-seven years of age; one woman, about forty-three, who is a good cook and washer, one woman about twenty-seven; and one very likely young woman, with three children. Also, at the same time and on the same terms, three MULES, about forty head of CATTLE, plantation tools, one wagon, and a first-rate Gin stand manufactured by Pratt & Co."[116] Another advertisement extolled: "Plantation on Red River, ten miles from Louisville [*sic*], Lafayette county, Arkansas, together with twenty-five likely and well-conditioned negroes for sale."[117] Joe Ray of Fulton witnessed slave auctions, in which enslaved men and women had to strip to the waist and submit to inspections. Buyers searched their potential purchases for scars from whippings; a lot of scars meant that the person was a probable flight risk or troublemaker.[118] Slave sales occurred whenever there was a need, though most slave sales were held in New Orleans or Memphis. There seemed to have been constant fear of being sold to speculators and thus torn from families.

The majority of enslaved people who lived in southwestern Arkansas were born in the states back east, as slavery existed in the area for about four decades only. The enslaved people of southwestern Arkansas lived in very primitive conditions, even if the plantation they worked generated a good income. Houses were usually log construction, one or two rooms deep, without windows; cotton bags filled with straw substituted for beds.[119] Food was served outside in troughs, and the cooking was done outside over open fires. Typical weekly allotments included salt meats or fat, molasses, corn meal, bran flour and milk.[120] Marriage, if the owner permitted it, was a very simple affair: the couple would simply move in together. Most enslaved peopled did not partake in rituals like birthdays, Thanksgiving or Christmas celebrations.

The differences in treatment of slaves between plantations could be profound. Some owner-families gave their enslaved people only leftovers from meals, but others made sure everyone got enough to eat.[121] Some enslaved people were never given the opportunity to go to church, while other plantation owners remained conscientiousness of their Christian duties.[122] Some enslaved people were not whipped, while others were thrashed simply because they had not received lashes in a while.[123] Sallie Crane, who was enslaved near Columbus in Hempstead County, remembered being whipped with cowhide and birch sprouts when she could not mind the many children she was in charge of and then having the cuts on her back mopped with a mixture of vinegar, salt and pepper to make them sting.[124] People who survived a severe lashing were tended by other slaves by being greased with lard and then wrapped tightly with sheets to make the bleeding stop and the blisters heal.[125]

The brutality of the southwestern frontier matched the harsh treatment that enslaved people endured. Their lot would change in 1865, when emancipation became a fact. However, African Americans would continue to feel the discriminating effects of a slave-based society for decades to come.

Chapter 2

Along the Southwest Trail

Crossroads for Nations

Between 1834 and 1835, an English geologist with the lavish name of G.W. Featherstonhaugh went on an extensive tour of the American slave states and found himself among the frenzy of pioneers descending onto southwestern Arkansas. He noted in his journal the rocks and soils of the state, but most of his colorful descriptions were reserved for the people of Arkansas. Near the Quachita River (he spelled it Washita), he was surprised to discover the brick house of the Barkmans, where he met with the lady of the house, whom everyone called She-Bear: "She chewed tobacco, she smoked a pipe, she drank whiskey, and cursed and swore as heartily as any backwoodsman."[126] Notwithstanding meeting this colorful character, Featherstonhaugh seemed pleasantly surprised by the beauty and fecundity of the Great Bend region. He found that southwestern Arkansas was "one of the most salubrious parts of Arkansas, and enjoys a temperate climate," with incredible beauty and fertility, "bearing extraordinary crops of cotton…gracefully surrounded by picturesque woods."[127]

Featherstonhaugh was less inclined to share the enthusiasm of so many people setting their sights for Texas. He wondered why "American citizens from great distances are constantly traversing [southwestern Arkansas] amidst all sorts of privations and difficulties, to seek a precarious existence in the unknown lands of Texas."[128] He took Dooley's ferry to see the promised land of Texas, then still part of Mexico. He described that the sandy banks were shifty, and the brambles and briars on the Texas bank of the Red River measured a foreboding twenty to thirty feet in height.

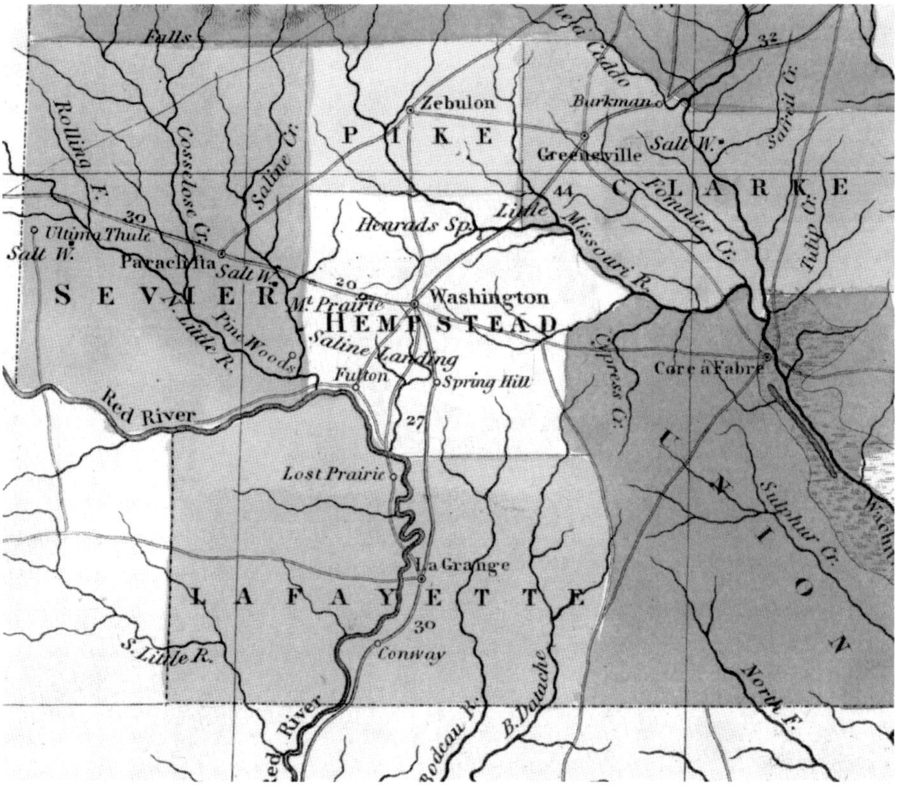

This 1847 map depicts the roads available to people traveling through or living in southwestern Arkansas. Washington is the connector for all of the routes. *Courtesy Library of Congress.*

Featherstonhaugh visited a Washington tavern where he may have seen Sam Houston, brooding over perceived injustices of Mexico against American settlers. He talked to men who had come back from Texas, where speculation and fraudulent land sales had ruined them financially. He noted the hypocrisy of the Texas-bound men who desired freedom and liberties for themselves but kept other humans as slaves.

What Featherstonhaugh witnessed was the essence of southwestern Arkansas in the period between statehood and the Civil War: boundless enthusiasm, surging populations, incredible growth and a land rife with revolution.

ROADS AND TRACES

By the 1830s, southwestern Arkansas had become a very popular destination. People had begun streaming into the Great Bend region to find new opportunities. Many came because they were forced to—the Choctaws, for example—and many came because they faced economic difficulties stemming from the depression of the late 1830s. Others came because new land beckoned and, with it, the chance to become self-sufficient farmers or even wealthy planters. A sizeable portion of immigrants were headed to Texas, a place where there was "no sich [*sic*] thing as a government there, and not one varmint of a lawyer in the hull place."[129]

Getting to this new "promised land" was an ordeal in itself. The road that led from Memphis to Little Rock had been constructed by the mid-1820s, and much of it was toll road. The extension into Washington in Hempstead County took a while longer but seemed to be relatively complete by the late 1820s. The road consisted merely of a sandy strip cut from the pines, sometimes reinforced with planks; logs set along shallow bottomlands; and private ferries assisting travelers in crossing larger streams. Today, the northern road out of Washington is indiscernible. The southern route, cut by private contractors and military personnel, is Arkansas State Road 195. This road—from Little Rock to Washington, then into Fulton—has become known as the Great Southwest Trail, though contemporaries never used that moniker. They instead described it as the Chihuahua Trail, as it led directly to Mexico. This trail became a kind of superhighway of the mid-nineteenth century.

With the building of Fort Towson in 1824, the layout of Fulton advertised in 1819 and again in 1829 and the establishment of a ferry crossing between Spring Hill and Rondo, the need to build better roads became very apparent. Two concerns occupied the territorial government: to appropriate funding for postal roads and to keep roads clear for military movement, which included the Choctaw and Chickasaw emigrant streams. Between 1834 and 1836, over $20,000 was appropriated to build roads from Washington to Fort Towson, Fulton, Dooley's Ferry, Jonesboro and Fort Smith.[130] A "national road" that would link Washington to Fort Towson and then into Texas was proposed by John Wilson, speaker of the House of Representatives, in 1833, but it was not completed.[131] In 1844, the Republic of Texas legislature authorized the survey of a "central national road" that ran from the Elm Fork of the Trinity River (today's Dallas) northeast to Jonesboro in order to link to the roads in Indian Territory and Arkansas, but this road never lived up to its promise either.

Edward Cross of Hempstead County worked as a surveyor, judge, U.S. representative and president of the Cairo and Fulton Railroad. He also met G.W. Featherstonhaugh on the Englishman's travels through southwestern Arkansas on the way to Mexico. *From the collections of the Arkansas Historical Commission.*

Military troops built roads to connect their stations to other forts. Along with daily muster drills, road building became a main function of soldiers along the southwestern frontier. This is why there are so many "military roads" throughout the region. While some of these roads used ancient trading paths that led to shallow crossings along rivers, many of the roads, such as the one from Washington to Fort Towson or from Washington to Fort Smith, originated with soldiers using saws, axes and hatches to clear narrow paths. Private contractors, using both slave and free labor, had the responsibility for building postal roads, such as the road from Washington to Fulton. At Fulton, the road split into separate paths. The road that was paid for by the Arkansas territorial government for use as a postal road went southeast to link to Spring Hill, Dooley's Ferry crossing and Lost Prairie across the Red River and was cut from an earlier Indian trade route. The trail that continued after a ferry crossing in Fulton at the Great Bend of the

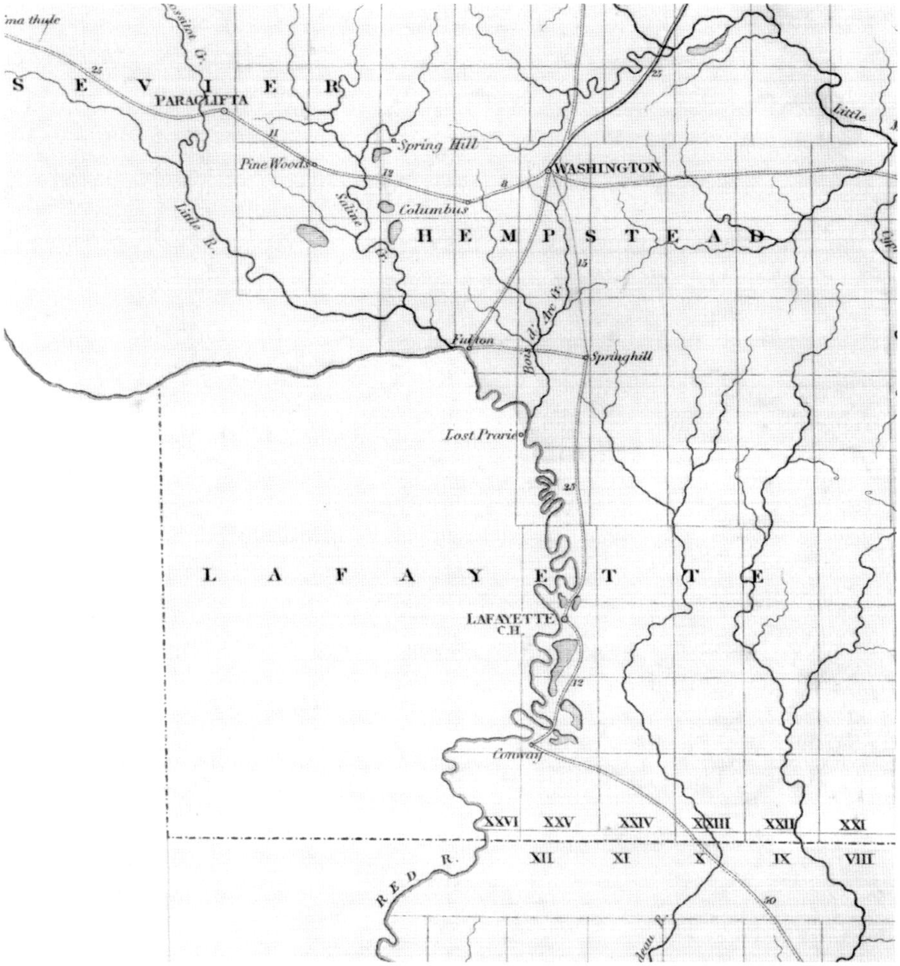

This map shows the location of Lafayette Courthouse, depicted as La Grange in other maps. The Lafayette County seat moved to Lewisville by the 1840s. Notice that there is a Springhill in Hempstead County and a Spring Hill in Sevier County. *Courtesy Library of Congress.*

Red River veered southwest as it entered Texas. Both routes would be known to locals as the Trammel's Trace.

Named after Nicholas Trammel, the trail was used by him and others as a way into or out of Texas. Nicholas Trammel's background has been shrouded in supposition, with some historians describing him as a horse smuggler and a swindler and others arguing that he had his hands in many enterprises, some of them actually legit. Whatever his purposes, he apparently established a route into the Missouri Territory as early as 1813 that linked to El Camino Real in Nacogdoches, partially using ancient Caddo paths. Another one of his trails linked Pecan Point and Jonesboro to Culbertson's Ferry at the Sulphur River. Men who would become legendary in the history of Texas used all of these roads and passed through some, if not most, of the settlements in southwestern Arkansas. The region acted almost like a funnel emptying into the vast, political powder keg that would become the twenty-eighth state.

GONE TO TEXAS

The troubles with the borders between Mexican Texas and the Arkansas Territory were not solved when Mexico decided to halt pursuing its claims to the southwestern part of Miller County in 1831. Instead, the nation's reluctance to enforce its territory actually gave brazen Americans the impetus to push the issue. When the Texans declared their independence from Mexico, several Miller County inhabitants signed the document. Richard Ellis, who owned a large plantation at Pecan Point and had been also invited to the Arkansas constitutional convention, served as president of the Texas convention. Robert Hamilton owned plantations near Lost Prairie and Pecan Point and was considered the wealthiest man at the convention. Collin McKinney claimed land filed under Benjamin Milam's Mexican grant and would later have a county and a county seat in Texas named after him. Albert H. Latimer founded a town called La Grange in today's Red River County, which briefly served as the seat for the newly formed Red River County after 1836. Samuel Carson lived in the western (and disputed) part of Lafayette County.[132]

After the revolution, the new Republic of Texas passed an act in 1838 that laid claim to the southwestern portion of Miller County.[133] While Arkansas, which had become a state in 1836, protested this action, it did not pursue it as vigorously as it could have. The state abolished Miller County in 1838, and a survey in 1841 set the boundaries where they are today.[134] The Arkansas portion of Miller County (east of the Index Line) became Lafayette County until a new Miller County was organized in 1874.

But not only Anglos sought adventure and fortune in Texas. Another Arkansas group found itself pushed into Texas, where it was not wanted—the Caddos.

By the 1830s, the Caddos had become part of a contingent of "roving Indians"—native people without a homeland, having been expelled from their ancestral lands due to disease, warfare or legal maneuvers. The different groups of the tribe who lived in southwestern Arkansas had consolidated to live under Kadohadacho leader Dehahuit first at the confluence of the Sulphur and Red Rivers and then in Natchitoches, Louisiana. The new Caddoan territory in northwestern Louisiana would not remain theirs for very long, as American treaties with other tribes, like the Quapaws, forced the Caddos to share their land. Their problems multiplied as annuities generated from the sale of tribal land were not paid, and many of the tribe members had to resort to begging and stealing after provisions ran out. When Americans began to lay claim to their lands, the Kadohadachos decided to sell their territory and remove to Mexican Texas, where they joined a band of Cherokees and their fellow Caddoans, the Hasinais, in 1835.[135]

The Kadohadachos, who numbered about five hundred, set up their village near Caddo Lake. This arrangement did not last long, either, as the Republic of Texas disregarded Mexican treaties with Indians. Once again, the Caddos found themselves landless and amid land-hungry, Indian-hating people. Stephen F. Austin, Robert Anderson Irion and James Pickney Henderson accused the Caddos of conspiring with Mexicans and committing depredations on white settlers.[136] John Forsyth, U.S. secretary of state, investigated the claims and found them warrantless. "The Caddoes [*sic*]…claim not to have committed any depredations on the whites," he wrote in a letter to Memucan Hunt, Texas minister to the United States, "and appear anxious to be on friendly terms with them."[137] The Texans insisted that the Caddos had become hostile and produced a journal found on the body of slain Mexican soldier Julian Pedro Miracle to substantiate their claims. The journal contained information that the Mexican government had promised land, ammunition and more to the Caddos, Cherokees, Kickapoos, Kichais, Wacos and Tehucanans if they agreed to fight the Texans.[138]

The Mexican plan did not pan out, and the United States military assisted the Texans in thwarting an attack. The Caddos consolidated into one tribe and declared peace with the Texans. They found refuge along the Brazos River, in present-day Hill County, from 1839 to 1854. Here, they farmed, built traditional villages and even assisted the Texans in apprehending renegade bands of Wacos and Wichitas who were not abiding by their own peace treaties. After 1854, the Caddos moved to the Brazos River Reservation in Young County. Because of growing Texan hostility against Indians due to continued raids conducted by Comanche tribes, the United

States leased land in Indian Territory and moved the Caddos to a new home by the Washita River in 1859. Upon fleeing to Kansas during the Civil War, the Caddos returned to the reservation that they shared with the Wichitas. After suffering further land loss due to the Dawes Severalty Act, the remaining Caddo Nation has made a permanent home in Caddo County, Oklahoma.[139] Today, they live in an arid western landscape, far removed from their Arkansas homelands of bayous, marshes and cypress groves.

EARLY PLACES IN THE GREAT BEND REGION

While it may be true in Europe when said that all roads lead to Rome, in southwestern Arkansas, all roads led to Washington. Marlbrook, near today's Blevins in northeastern Hempstead County, served as the first location of the county courthouse—court was held inside the home of John English—but Washington became the commercial and then governmental center.[140] The town site, formerly a place for revivals known as Ebenezer Campground, was chosen in 1824 because it sat on high ground and on the right of way for the extension of the military road from Little Rock to Fulton.[141] A few settlers, such as Elijah Stuart, had already begun farming there by 1818, and Elijah's tavern became the heart of the town as an inn for travelers as well as a stagecoach stop and early post office. A two-story, hand-hewn building, the tavern was described by G.W. Featherstonhaugh as a dark and dirty place but apparently well visited. Along with his possible sighting of Sam Houston, the tavern may have played host to the likes of Davy Crockett, Benjamin Milam, Stephen F. Austin, John Neely Bryan (the founder of Dallas) and James Bowie. Both James Bowie and Stephen F. Austin had close ties to Washington: James Bowie commissioned his eponymous knife from the local blacksmith, and Stephen F. Austin served as a territorial judge at Washington in 1821 after closing his provision store for his Mexico-bound settlers at Long Prairie.[142]

By 1826, the townspeople organized Washington into a sizeable village, with several hotels, saloons and mercantile stores catering to its citizens and the many travelers who came. Most of the early passersby were on their way to Texas or to the new lands in Indian Territory; in the 1840s, prospectors swept through town on their way to the California gold rush. A Jewish family settled in town as well. Washington proved to be a busy place during the Mexican-American War of 1846, when troops passed through on their way to

By mid-century, downtown Washington was a bustling place. Cattle, donkeys, horses and men shared the road. *From the collections of the Arkansas Historical Commission.*

Fort Towson and Fort Washita in Indian Territory, and a volunteer army was mustered there. During the Civil War, Washington became the Confederate capital of Arkansas after the Union army took control of Little Rock in 1863.[113]

The *Washington Telegraph*, published by William H. Etter, an "ardent Whig," became the major source of news in southwestern Arkansas in 1840.[114] Several protestant congregations formed churches in the town, and Washington also boasted separate academies for boys and girls, sponsored either by a church or by subscription. It was only after Reconstruction that schools were financed through public taxes. The first black public school opened in 1871 inside a Baptist church, with the white public high school opening in 1873.[115] Washington also boasted a horse racetrack and the Liberty Campground, which hosted revivals, and served as a stop for at least two stagecoach lines.[116]

Homes built by the early settlers were usually in the typical American pioneer style of the dogtrot house—a two-room cabin with a low roof, divided by a central breezeway. Some were mere shacks; others were cozy and inviting. G.W. Featherstonhaugh recalled visiting the home of Edward Cross, an early settler of Hempstead County whose varied career included positions as a surveyor, plantation overseer, territorial judge, congressman, Supreme Court judge, Arkansas attorney general and the president of the Cairo and Fulton Railroad. According to Featherstonhaugh, Edward Cross and his wife, a relative of Stephen F. Austin, welcomed visitors in their house near today's Blevins, where they entertained in a comfortable home that sported a rare rug on the floor, a warm fireplace and—surprise!—a piano. As pioneers turned into successful farmers, planters or merchants, their homes reflected their status. Dogtrot breezeways were enclosed with doors framed in the Greek revival style of broad wooden trims and geometric scrollwork. The commercial buildings in the downtowns were often erected with whitewashed clapboard siding; the more substantial buildings were constructed of brick and generally housed local banks. The typical "big houses," with their Doric columns and impressive porches that tend to be associated with large plantations, were rarely evident in the Great Bend region, though Hugh Blevins's home northeast of Washington boasted a curved staircase and was arguably one of the most impressive houses in the country. The settlements of Columbus and Spring Hill also featured their fair share of two-story homes with balconies and porches. Despite the elegance of the residences of the wealthy, most of the houses owned by mechanics, overseers and yeoman farmers were relatively unadorned, with only a few sporting porches and generally only one story tall. Slave quarters tended to be simple, primitive cabins, many with dirt floors. Poor whites—those of European background who owned neither slaves nor land and who hired out their labor—also lived in small cabins or simple dugouts. Invariably, kitchens were built away from the sleeping quarters to keep fire danger at a minimum. In town, businessmen built homes that were destined to impress, with imported decorations and tidy gardens. Homes situated along the Southwest Trail saw plenty of visitors, according to Sam Williams. "In the early days, houses were scarce stopping places, few and far inbetween the public highways," he noted in his memoir of southwestern Arkansas, *Printer's Devil*. "There was hardly a house on the roadside that would not entertain way-farers." During the mass migration into Texas following the creation of the republic, sixty visitors per night was apparently not uncommon.[147]

The abundant timber in the region led to the construction of mostly wooden homes, with flag- or sandstone fireplaces. Sadly, upkeep of the labor-intensive materials at times proved difficult, and many of the early homes in the region were razed to make way for mid-twentieth-century brick homes.

George Dooley received exclusive permission to operate his ferry across Red River in 1834, and while he sold the landing within two years, his

Fulton, founded in 1819 and situated in a prime location at the Great Bend of the Red River, became a prominent riverboat center. *From the collections of the Arkansas Historical Commission.*

name became forever associated with the crossing. Located along an ancient Indian shallow-water crossing twelve miles below Fulton, Dooley's Ferry became the easiest, fastest and relatively most comfortable way to cross into Texas. Dooley's ferry operators had to defend themselves against malicious rumors made by competing ferry operators, though, who claimed that the road to Dooley's was in bad repair.[148] During the Civil War, Dooley's Ferry carried state records across the river for safe storage in Rondo, and Confederate troops built fortifications and trenches to protect this important river crossing from the Union army. By 1937, the ferry was no longer in operation, as roads and free bridges made its function obsolete. Today, the ferry site is no longer accessible to the public, and its exact location is open for debate. Dooley's ferry landing seems to be situated on the east bank of the Red River between the First and Second Old River Lakes. Travelers can get near it by taking Miller County Road 379 or Hempstead County Roads 7 and 155.

Spring Bank, a small settlement along the Red River on a high bluff just below the Sulphur River confluence, was the site of a ferry operated by the

Blantons, one of southwestern Arkansas' earliest families. Situated near the old Sulphur River Indian Factory, Spring Bank had a post office, wharf, several plantation landings, docks, a sawmill and some stores.[149]

Fulton was the home of two important ferry crossings. Situated at the confluence of the Red and Little Rivers, the town of Fulton grew into an important commercial center by the mid-nineteenth century, with a deepwater crossing across the Red River and Allen's Ferry across the Little River. An advertisement looking to sell town lots, placed in the *Arkansas Gazette* in 1819, described Fulton as being "handsomely situated on the north east bank of main Red River, about two miles below the mouth of Little Red River, and near the center of the boundary of Arkansas Territory on Red River. It is the principal landing and place of deposit, for the county of Hempstead, and is also the point at which the most direct road leading from Missouri territory, and many of the eastern states, to the extensive and fertile province of Texas, will cross said river."[150] Fulton was originally platted as a speculation scheme between Major Hyde, Edward Cross, Roswell Beebe and Thomas S. Boles. According to Sam Williams, trouble may have brewed if Fulton had grown into a city, as Enoch J. Smith claimed much of the town lot through the Preemptive Homestead Act and probably would have sued for trespass.[151] By 1839, Daniel Marble built a hotel to accommodate travelers seeking passage into Texas, but its location at the Great Bend of the Red River created Fulton's main purpose as a steamboat landing. In fact, Fulton became "one of the most important river towns on the Red River…it formed the gateway to the Southwest."[152] The town saw a variety of travelers, who could dine at the Cross Keys or Union taverns and spend the night at several boardinghouses and hotels erected to serve them. Fulton regaled its visitors with a bowling alley, gambling halls, saloons and a candy store, but it also meant business by erecting several warehouses to store cotton for the trip downriver.[153] Churches were not prominently featured in a town that was geared toward commerce. "The people of Fulton," Sam Williams opined, "were not, as a rule, religiously inclined."[154]

Lost Prairie also served as a gateway to the southwest, albeit briefly. Home to several plantations, it was granted a post office in 1828, but its location in the lands west of the Red River, across from Dooley's Ferry, also placed it squarely in the territory disputed with Mexico. Benjamin Milam lived and conducted business here, but not for too long, as he followed Stephen F. Austin, who at one point lived at Long Prairie, to seek adventure in Texas. Spring Hill, located east of the Red River between Washington and Lewisville, fared better. It became home to male and female boarding schools and was lauded in an advertisement posted in the *Arkansas Gazette* as "one of the most healthy settlements in the south, or south west…The springs are abundant, and the water of the most excellent quality."[155] Wealthy planters from Virginia, who decided to move to southwestern Arkansas to take advantage of the fertile soil that seemed so conducive to producing cotton, settled in Spring Hill, where wealth came to rely on a booming slave trade and gentility was cultivated in its renowned, subscription-based academies. Another wealthy enclave was Columbus, located a few miles due west of Washington along the military road. Founded by Samuel Moren of Missouri in 1819, Columbus boasted the first gristmill in the county and had a post office by 1834.[156] Between Washington and Columbus sat Mound Prairie, which was first settled by Abraham Stuart in 1818[157] and named after a Caddoan burial mound that is now part of Rick Evans Grandview Prairie Wildlife Management Area. Ozan and Saline Landing, just north of Columbus and Mound Prairie, were also early settlements. Saline Landing sat along the Little River and was "the shipping point for all the country around Columbus…Several thousand bales of cotton were annually shipped from there to New Orleans."[158] According to Sam Williams's memoir, John Johnson built a steamboat at Saline Landing. Today, the town's original site is under Millwood Lake.

Chickaninny Prairie has been deemed the location of Lafayette County's first courthouse. That distinction was then given to La Grange, situated near James Sevier Conway's Walnut Hill Plantation, where a log cabin served the judicial circuit. The official seat of Lafayette County was transferred in 1841 to Lewisville, a small settlement named after a prominent planter. Town boosters for Lewisville began selling plats through the *Arkansas Gazette* and had nothing but good things to say about this new town: "Lewisville is situated upon that beautiful undulating, elevated pine ridge…the vicinity has proven to be almost uninterruptedly healthy for the last six years…surrounded by up and bottom lands of the first order—by bold and never failing springs of pure freestone water; and a most delightful climate—accessible from any and every point, is unquestionably desirable both for the merchant, mechanic, or private resident."[159] Nearby Garland City, named either after investor Rufus Garland or his uncle Josiah, was established around 1833 as a prominent ferry crossing and steamship mooring.[160] Several other small villages were founded along the Red River, such as Rocky Comfort, Richmond, Pine Prairie, Wallace, Peytonville and Laynesport, which was established by an Irish family. Rocky Comfort and Richmond were also settled by Irish immigrants, as well as American emigrants from Kentucky, Tennessee and Missouri.[161] Their relatively isolated location made for good hideouts for people escaping civilization and the law. H.M. McIver, a longtime Rocky

Comfort resident, told of an attorney named "Bee" Smith who had run away from New Orleans after an altercation with and subsequent murder of a "carpetbagger" attorney. He later surrendered but did not serve any jail time, as witnesses could no longer be found. Bee Smith rediscovered his long-lost love in Louisiana and returned with her to southwestern Arkansas to live out the remainder of his days.[162] The villages of Rocky Comfort, Richmond, Pine Prairie, Wallace, Peytonville and Laynesport became part of Little River County when it was formed from Hempstead and Servier Counties in 1867. They existed mainly because of the river, which grew into a major commercial outlet from the 1830s to the 1890s.

COMMERCE ALONG THE GREAT BEND

The first steamboat to journey through the Red River in southwestern Arkansas was a small, lightweight ship named the *Enterprise* (formerly known as the *Alps*), which plied the Little River and Red River from Saline Landing to Fort Towson amid much fanfare: "Her arrival created great rejoicings among the citizens residing above the Raft, on both sides of the river."[163] Benjamin Milam was a passenger on the ship that passed Lost Prairie on the June 18, 1831. While he said that navigation was possible, he recommended to the *Gazette* that the Great Raft, which clogged the river above Natchitoches, Louisiana, be removed to allow more boats to come through.[164] For years, the "Great Raft" had been a thorn in the sides of the governors of Louisiana and Arkansas Territory, the military commanders at Fort Towson and the U.S. Army Corps of Engineers.

Created by an immense, centuries-old logjam, the Great Raft made navigation into Arkansas from points south extremely difficult. As the flat, fertile fields surrounding the river in the territory proved to be good cotton country, and provisions needed to be shipped to Fort Towson in Indian Territory, the federal government decided that the raft needed to be removed to establish a water highway. The removal, which would be overseen on the federal level by the secretary of war, became Captain Henry Shreve's responsibility.

At first, the U.S. Army Corps of Engineers recommended the building of a series of canals to circumvent the obstruction in 1831, but Speaker of House William Timble rejected the idea. Timble emphasized that "the importance of this subject is of great magnitude...the counties of Hempstead, Servier, Lafayette, and Miller are wholly dependent on the Red River as their only navigation" and that anything less than the logjam removal would be cost

The steam ship *Packet Home*, based out of Yazoo City, docked at Fulton in the 1860s. *From the collections of the Arkansas Historical Commission.*

prohibitive and wreak havoc on trade. "Should our prayer not be granted," Timble continued, "this fine region of country, which would otherwise be the flower of the West and the pride of our Territory, must ultimately depopulate and dwindle into insignificance."[165] Congress appropriated $25,000 for the operation. Captain Henry Shreve, a seasoned riverboat captain who had earlier cleared jams on the Arkansas and Mississippi Rivers, brought his snag boats to the Red River to start eating the deadfall, and by 1833, sixty miles of the raft had already been removed. Estimating that trade along the Red River could reach $300,000 per year if the waters became navigable, Congress readily agreed to continue funding the operation.

The Great Raft removal proved not an easy task. Shreve's crew, which numbered around 160, had caught cholera during an Ohio River obstruction removal. Thus, he had difficulty recruiting more help. His snag boats made the operation a little easier, however. Shreve patented a type of snag boat that ground the timber on the ship and then spewed the chips into the water. His boats, the *Heliopolis* and *Archimedes*, became the standard bearers of subsequent water maintenance vessels. The centuries-old trees that Shreve and his men removed were waterlogged and rock hard, making the task

Cotton proved to be the main commercial export for people in southwestern Arkansas. The cotton-based economy fostered plantations and slavery. The *Waukesha* docked with a full load at Fulton in this undated photo. *From the collections of the Arkansas Historical Commission.*

difficult and dangerous, and the summer heat did not help their progress any, either. Nonetheless, Shreve found the Red River job "fortunate," as cholera and other illnesses did not waylay the crew, as once happened in the Arkansas River. The climate surrounding the Red River, Shreve surmised, was beneficial.[166]

There was a darker side to the Great Raft removal. The swamps and bayous created by the logjam sustained fish, alligators, panthers, bears, birds and other diverse wildlife, but this biodiversity was extinguished when the snag boats made short shrift of the logs. Flowers and plants indigenous to the Red River Valley vanished, many never having been catalogued. The destruction of this natural phenomenon ruined a unique ecosystem and also changed two cultures: the Caddos and the French Creoles of Natchitoches. For centuries, the Caddos had relied on the backlog of water from the jam to fertilize their cornfields. Having a steady source of water in an area that could experience extended periods of drought was immensely beneficial and may have been the impetus for their highly complex civilization. Another civilization that relied on the logjam was the plantation culture along the Red River near Natchitoches. For several years, keelboats were sent downstream, and steamboats came upstream from New Orleans to be laden with cotton, indigo and tobacco from the planter's private piers and chutes that lined the many channels of the river. Once the Great Raft was cleared, the Red River became narrower and straighter, and plantations suddenly found themselves about a mile or so away from the new riverbed. Crops had to be carried by land to the new river ports, and for a while, it seemed that Natchitoches' days were numbered. On the flipside, Shreveport was founded, named in honor of Captain Shreve, who was also an investor in the city. Shreveport and Jefferson, Texas, established in 1844, would both become inland port cities and greatly benefit from the initial clearing of the raft.

Captain Shreve urged Congress to continue funding cleanup of the Red River lest the jam occur again. His pleas were not heeded, however; budgetary constraints and economic troubles—such as the economic depression of 1836 after the National Bank was not renewed—left maintenance coffers empty. A letter to the editor of the *Arkansas Gazette* revealed the urgency to keep the river clear a mere ten years after Captain Shreve completed the first clearing. The writer complained that cotton cost several times more per bale for planters who lived along the Red River than for planters on the Arkansas River due to the extra amount of time it took to navigate the clogged waters. Further, according to the anonymous letter writer, southwestern Arkansas would remain unsettled and impermanent if the Great Raft was not cleared, as internal improvements would not be forthcoming if transportation remained unreliable.[167] The last jams of the Great Raft were ultimately removed through a series of ill-planned nitroglycerin charges in the 1870s. The Red River shifted its course, and the big Cypress Bayou that sustained Jefferson shrunk and could no longer support paddle-wheelers and steamboats. Jefferson, by then the seat of Cass County, lost its economic importance as a river city.

The people of southwestern Arkansas celebrated the raft's removal, of course. An article in the *Arkansas Gazette* dated March 21, 1838, read:

> *By last Friday evening's mail, we received a letter from a respectable merchant at Washington, dated 14th inst., giving us the highly gratifying and certain intelligence, that a passage has been effected through the Great Raft of Red River—that two steam boats have passed up through the opening—and that one of them (the* Indian*) arrived at Fulton, on the 13th, laden with merchandize and other supplies, for the merchants, &c. residing above that hitherto great obstruction to the navigation of Red River. We congratulate our fellow citizens of the south on the pleasing prospect*

Snag boats, like the *C.W. Howell* on Spirit Lake, were common sights when the Red River was still navigable. These vessels cleared debris and jams from the channel. *From the collections of the Arkansas Historical Commission.*

> *they now have of soon possessing an open and unobstructed channel through which to send the rich products of their fertile soil to the great commercial market of the valley of the Mississippi.*[168]

When a group of 180 recruits from New York easily made their way to Fort Towson via the Red River in April of 1838, "in less than half the time it was ever done before," the future of southwestern Arkansas seemed assured.[169]

With the Red River now easily navigable, Garland City, Fulton, Laynesport and Jonesboro became prominent commercial centers in the Great Bend region. Proprietor B.H. Layne praised his nascent town of Laynesport in the *Arkansas Gazette* when he advertised lots for sale, describing the site as "8 or 10 feet above high water mark…it being the only good crossing or even landing place on the North side of the river, for 30 or 40 miles up or down…it [is] a place not to be excelled, or perhaps equaled, by any town on our Southern inland waters."[170] Steamboats plied the waters, mostly to transport cotton and passengers. Ships would dock weekly, if not daily, at these cities, with one ship going as far west as Arthur City, Lamar County, Texas. An incomplete steamship roster, gleaned from newspaper accounts and assorted recollections, included the *Caspian* (1838), the *Napoleon* (1844), *Frontier* (1844), *Colonel Harvey* (1844), *Miami* (1844), *Waverly* (1844), *Douglass* (1844), *Campte* (1846), *Southwestern* (1846), the *Little River* (1847), *Jim Gilmer* (1847 and 1848), *Franklin* (1847), *Buffalo* (1848), *General Butler* (1848), *A.B. Shaw* (1848) and the *Belle of Illinois* (1847 and 1848). Accidents happened, as well: the steamers *Marmion* and *Amelia* sank near Pecan Point in 1841 and 1848, respectively, and the *Texarkana* sank in 1870 with whiskey on board.[171] Toward the end of the steamboat era, a few ships were retained for simple excursion cruises. The *Rosa Bland*, for example, steamed weekly from Fulton to Laynesport in 1891, decked in electric lights.[172]

The railroads gradually lessened the need for steamboats, and by the turn of the twentieth century, the Red River was once again a silent stream. Sandbars have retaken the channel, and today its waterways are used only by recreational boaters and fishermen.

THE CIVIL WAR ALONG THE GREAT BEND

When Arkansas seceded from the Union in May 1861, discontent with the Union had not been the prime mover for this action. While Arkansas had pledged itself through the practice of slavery to be a thoroughly Southern state, it joined the Confederacy not because of non-enforcement of the fugitive slave acts (which South Carolina claimed) or that its borders were not being properly defended (as Texas pointed out). Instead, Arkansas seceded as a matter of principal and allegiance to its southern roots—the United States had declared war on the other states that had already seceded, and to submit to this "inhuman design…would be disgraceful and ruinous to the State of Arkansas."[173] The "war between the states" in Arkansas was relatively short, however; most of Arkansas came under Union control already by 1863.

Citizens of Hempstead County and Lafayette County, the two counties that encompassed the Great Bend region during this period, gathered in front of their respective courthouses on January 26, 1861, to vote to either stay or leave the Union. Hempstead County voted to remain, and Lafayette County voted to secede, but like most counties in Arkansas, Texas and Indian Territory that hugged the Red River, it went to war when Arkansas' legislature announced secession. Men from several families in the counties at first volunteered their

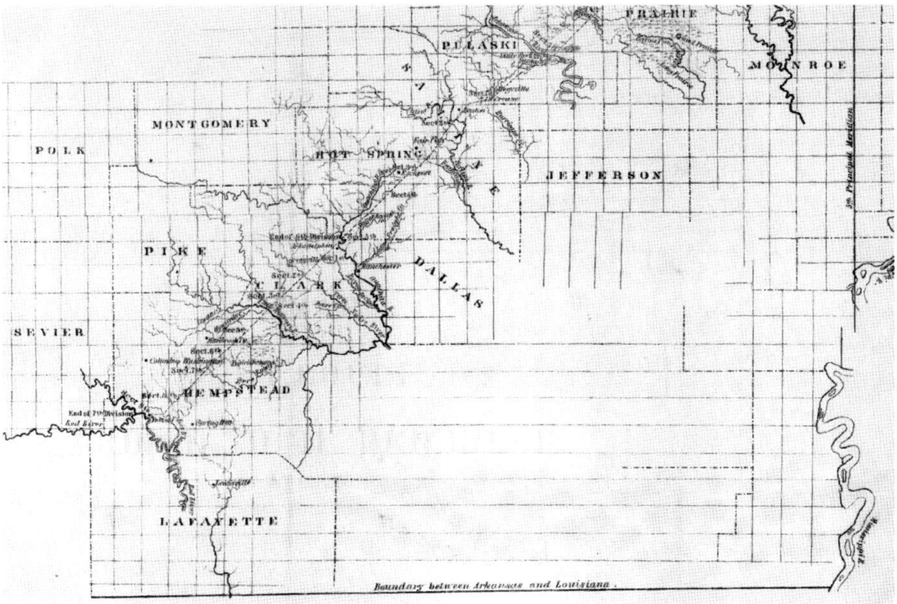

A surveyed route from St. Louis to Fulton by Joshua Barney is depicted in this 1852 map. *From the collections of the Arkansas Historical Commission.*

service. When the war proved to become a much longer and violent affair, Arkansas began to conscript soldiers, and several draftees came from families who lived in the Great Bend region. The following list is in no way exhaustive but does demonstrate just how committed southwestern Arkansas was to the cause. Hempstead County organized many companies: the First, Eighth and Sixty-ninth Militia Brigades (the First Militia Brigade was commanded by Brigadier General Benjamin P. Jett of Washington); the Fourth Arkansas Infantry Regiment, Companies B and E (Evander McNair from Hempstead County commanded the regiment); the Sixth Calvary, Company D; the Twentieth Arkansas Infantry, Companies A, B and E; and the Second Mounted Rifles, Company H. Lafayette County contributed several men as well: the Fourth Arkansas Infantry Regiment, Company D; the Fifteenth Arkansas Infantry, Company F; and the Twentieth Arkansas Infantry, Company K. Several of the companies engaged in battles as far away as Missouri.

Like most of Arkansas, the Great Bend region witnessed chaos during the conflict between the states and dealt with the calamities of war as best it could. In Washington, several churches and the school became hospitals for wounded soldiers, with the resident ladies tending to the wounded.

Area women also formed sewing circles to construct Confederate uniforms and helped to raise $23,000 to support the families of soldiers, many of whom became destitute as planting and harvesting were suspended during the war. Local citizens also paid the property taxes of soldiers who were unable to. Confederate soldiers encamped at Camp Sumter near Spring Hill were entertained by ladies from Washington, Spring Hill, Columbus and Lewisville with religious revivals, dances to raise funds and enthusiastic parades. The editor of the *Washington Telegraph*, John R. Eakin, kept publishing his newspaper with the help of citizens, who donated food, paper and candles to maintain communication with the outside world.[174]

An underlying sense of fear and uncertainty manifested itself in violence in southwestern Arkansas. Runaway slaves were hanged to thwart possible insurrections.[175] Refugees and renegade soldiers deserting their posts overran Washington. Several plantations moved their slaves to leased land in Texas to continue their operations, thus emptying the region of food and manpower.[176] The resulting food shortages and forced conscription led to much anger, especially among poor whites. In Lewisville, women raided stores to feed their hungry children.[177] Soap was in short supply, and drinking water looked "muddier than the Red River when swollen."[178] Roving bands of soldiers, "bushwhackers" and "jayhawks" began to forage for food and supplies, raiding the remaining farms and plantations. Although accounts after the war by local citizens blamed the raids on Union soldiers, much of the destruction was apparently perpetrated by Confederate forces. H.M. McIver from Rocky Comfort recounted that "Yankee General Gano" had raided the area and took horses, mules, wagons and cows. However, he may have been remembering Confederate brigadier general Richard M. Gano of Kentucky, who, as part of Sam Bell Maxey's command, was encamped at Laynesport in 1864.[179]

When Union forces penetrated Arkansas after the Camden campaign in 1863, Washington became the state capital of Arkansas to thwart occupation. Charles T. Anderson of Fulton, who took his father's place during conscription, assisted in removing the state archives from Hot Springs to Washington, traveling "all night with the Yanks after us."[180] The records were then transferred to Rondo, across the Red River, for safekeeping. To prevent possible Union destruction of the records—and to stop potential invasion into Texas and Louisiana—the Tenth Arkansas Calvary under John B. Magruder built fortifications and trenches east of Dooley's Ferry landing and possibly a prisoner-of-war holding pen.[181] Ultimately, the battle at Prairie d'Ane of April 1864, east of Washington in today's Nevada County, halted the Union campaign in southwest Arkansas. Union general Steele planned an invasion of Shreveport, which he hoped to do after joining forces with several infantry and cavalry forces that were coming up the Red River from Natchitoches. Unluckily for him, Union troops were defeated at Mansfield in northeastern Louisiana. Steele's troops were defeated themselves by Confederate soldiers under General Sterling Price. The aforementioned soldier Charles T. Anderson and his fellow troops built breastworks at Prairie d'Ane and years later recounted the protracted battle. According to his account, over 650 "hungry, half-clothed" Confederate Choctaw forces of the Second Indian Brigade, commandeered by Colonel Tandy Walker, assisted in the fight. The two-day battle, which included a skirmish at Jenkins Ferry, ended when the Union army turned back toward Camden. The Southern troops followed the retreating Northern soldiers to Poison Springs, where, according to Anderson, "the Indians fought the [Union soldier] Negroes—killing and scalping them… [the dead] were so thick that you could walk on them."[182] Southwestern Arkansas, Louisiana and Texas remained in Southern hands until the end of the war. In September 1864, the Arkansas legislature convened in Washington, where funds were appropriated for the safe storage of the state archives, to support indigent families and to buy medicine and machinery. The legislature also voted to extend the death penalty for many infractions, including "slave stealing"—this may have been a response to the Emancipation Proclamation and the practice of Union troops in enlisting enslaved people for service.[183]

During this tumultuous time, the *Arkansas Gazette* and *Washington Telegraph* recommended destroying roads and storing cotton in isolated outbuildings to protect homes in case the Union army marched through. Peace societies and even pro-Union sentiment began to build. Citizens around the Great Bend were becoming war-weary and disillusioned. When Jefferson Davis was captured in May 1865, the *Arkansas Gazette* reported rejoicing and relief and blamed the whole mêlée on ill-guided politicians.[184] In June of that year, the Twelfth Michigan Infantry entered Washington. The *Washington Telegraph* stated, "At noon last Wednesday, our citizens beheld a novel sight…the old flag of the United States, borne in with a band of music, and waving over the heads of the 12th Michigan veteran Infantry. They were received by our people in the right manner, and nothing has occurred to disturb the harmony." Reading the account, one could almost hear a sigh of relief when the editorial ended with: "The four year struggle was finally over."[185]

The end of the Civil War marked the end of a volatile era in American history. The periods of time following the conflict—Reconstruction, industrialization and the modern eras—completely changed the landscape of southwestern Arkansas.

Chapter 3

Along the Railroads

New Ways

During the depression of the 1930s, the Works Progress Administration (WPA), a relief agency established under Franklin Delano Roosevelt, created an assignment called the Federal Writers' Project. Writers, teachers, scholars and other unemployed "learned folk" were hired to collect cultural, economic, historical and social information about the inhabitants of the forty-eight states. Because the agency had been tacked onto the WPA as an afterthought, its purpose was not too clear, but eventually, the many people who assisted in developing the endeavor created a documentary history of the United States by compiling interviews with citizens who recounted historical events, regional recipes, photographs, folktales, religious practices and local music. One of the missions of the Federal Writers' Project was for correspondents to interview former slaves. Men and women, ancient in the 1930s but young at the time of emancipation, recollected the tribulations and successes in their antebellum lives and beyond. One of the interviewees was Katie Rowe, who lived in Tulsa, Oklahoma, but grew up in Hempstead County.

Ms. Rowe was interviewed by Robert Vinson Lackey, who attempted to retain her native dialect in his transcriptions. Ms. Rowe remembered the day that she learned that she had been emancipated. Coming from the fields to the sound of the horn in the middle of the afternoon, she and the other enslaved people, all toiling as the property of Dr. Isaac Jones of Washington, gathered around the porch of the overseer's house. After the overseer called roll, Ms. Rowe noticed a man sitting "on de gallery in a hide-bottom chair…a man we never see before." The man told them that on this day, the fourth of

June, 1865, "Today you is free, jest lak I is." He explained to Ms. Rowe and the others that "you don't have to git up and go by de horn no more. You is your own bosses now...I wants to bless you and hope you always is happy, and tell you got all de right and life dat any white people got."[186]

Katie Rowe never learned the name of the man who told her she was free, but she stated, "It was the fourth day of June in 1865 that I begins to live, and I gwine take de picture of dat old man...clean into my grave wid me."[187] She became a sharecropper and then lived in the city before eventually farming with her husband on their own land in Indian Territory. Her story illustrated many attributes of the post–Civil War period in southwestern Arkansas: navigating her way in a new, unchartered world.

RECONSTRUCTING THE GREAT BEND REGION

The Civil War may have not placed many scars on the physical landscape of the Red River Valley in southwestern Arkansas, but it did leave a legacy of racial tensions. Emancipation proved to be easy enough to add to the new state constitutions Arkansas had to write upon defeat (the first Reconstruction constitution, passed in 1864, outlawed slavery; the second one in 1868 included black male suffrage; and the final one of 1874 severely limited state powers in favor of local governments) but much harder to implement as Arkansas reverted back to its southern Democrat roots.

Upon emancipation, some freedmen and freedwomen left the plantations as soon as they could; others stayed on to continue to work the farms, often as sharecroppers. Others were "turned out" as soon as the war ended, without compensation or provisions, while yet other former slaves were deeded plots of land, mules and seed. The Freedmen's Bureau in Arkansas reported of threats made to former slaves if they filed complaints against white landowners who refused to pay them for their labor. Emancipated children who did not have immediate family were apprenticed to their former owners under the oversight of the Freedmen's Bureau. Harriet Norwood, a nine-year-old orphan girl from Washington in Hempstead County, was apprenticed to William G. John "to learn the art of housekeeping" until her eighteenth birthday. Mr. John was also supposed to teach her reading, writing and arithmetic.[188]

The Reconstruction era has often been seen as a period of lawlessness in southern histories. Newspapers from the late 1860s and into the 1870s

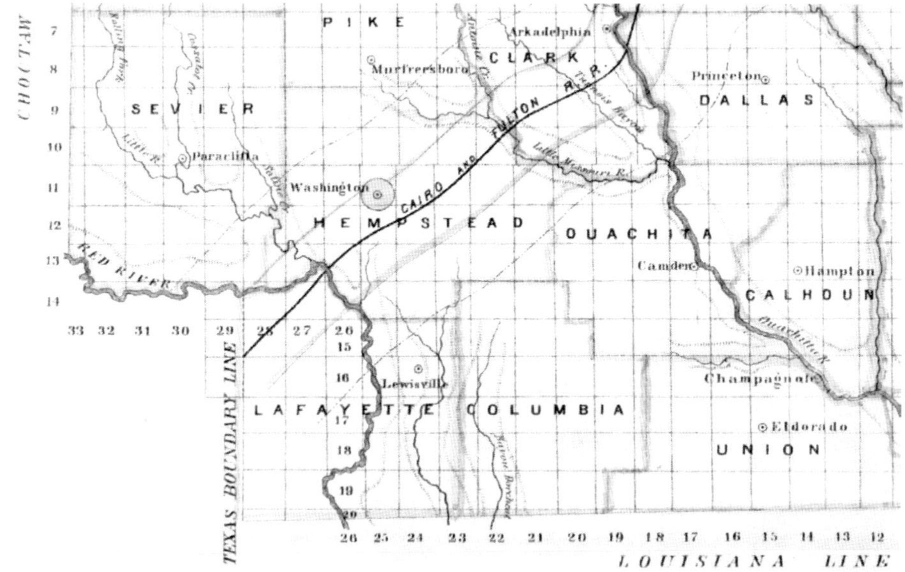

Joshua Barney's surveyed route would become the proposed right of way for the Cairo and Fulton Railroad. While investors dreamt of laying tracks in the 1850s, the railroad would not become a reality until 1873. *Courtesy Library of Congress.*

recounted multiple murders. The *Washington Telegraph* reported a "Negro mob" beating and stoning a white man in April 1872 and a shooting at the courthouse a few days after.[189] The story of Cullen Baker helps to illustrate the violence of this era. Baker was an ardent southern Democrat and Ku Klux Klan member who despised Republican rule in Arkansas, the Freedman's Bureau and emancipation. A Confederate veteran who once deserted his regiment and then left his second post due to a disability, Baker funded his vigilantism through robberies, tributes by his fellow gang members and the friendliness of some plantation owners. Doc Quinn, a freedman from Texarkana, joined Baker's gang for protection against anti-Democrat sentiment. Quinn explained that as a Democratic voter, he faced possible assault by other freedmen, who were predominantly Republican. Quinn recounted how he once saved Baker's life during a high-water crossing on the Red River near Fulton, becoming Baker's faithful servant thereafter. To assist Baker, Quinn rounded up freedmen under the pretext of forming "a colored militia to catch Cullen Baker and his gang." Instead, Quinn delivered the freedmen to Baker, who would "shoot them by the score," killing fifty-three at Homan; eighty-six at Rocky Comfort; six at Ogden; sixty-two in Jefferson, Texas; one hundred in northern Louisiana;

Frances Black toiled as a slave in southwestern Arkansas until emancipation. She lived in Texarkana until her death, where she was interviewed for the Federal Writers' Project. *Courtesy Library of Congress.*

and seventy-three at Marshall, Texas.[190] Baker and his gang were accused of killing "Major Andrews, Lieutenant Willis, and an unknown colored man" in Little River County.[191] Baker would later be killed by his romantic rival, Thomas Orr.[192]

Like most southern states, the Ku Klux Klan organized in Arkansas in the Reconstruction era. Washington was home to one of the "dens," or meeting places, for its secret chapter.[193] The Klan was responsible for voter intimidation, countless unsolved murders of citizens and officials and vigilante lynchings. Arkansas governor Powell Clayton, the first Republican to hold that office, called for a state militia in Hempstead, Little River (founded in 1867) and Lafayette Counties, which were "in a state of insurrection" due to Klan activities.[194] This order created the military districts that ruled Arkansas between 1868 and 1876. Southwestern Arkansas came under the authority of Brigadier General Robert F. Catterson.[195] While the *Washington Telegraph* insisted that the militia was not needed and groused at the "colored militia" that paraded through town in 1871 and the many "carpetbaggers" who had swarmed into the town, military rule stayed in effect. Clayton Powell faced impeachment in 1871, but Republican rule over Arkansas did not end until 1874, when Augustus Hill Garland, whose father was the namesake of Garland City, became

Arkansas' "redeemer" governor. He was raised in Washington and worked as an attorney there. After his service in the Civil War and a pardon from President Andrew Johnson, he returned to his law practice in Washington. As an ex-Confederate, he was denied access to the Supreme Court, and he successfully sued to restore the constitutional right. As governor, Garland, a Democrat, reduced the debt left behind by the Clayton and supported educational expansion. Reconstruction did not officially end in the South until the infamous "election deal" of 1877. Rutherford B. Hayes, who needed a few more electoral votes to win the U.S. presidency against Samuel Tilden, apparently negotiated for the votes with representatives from South Carolina, Florida and Louisiana. In return, Hayes lifted military Reconstruction, and Arkansas quickly reverted back to a predominantly Democrat-ruled government.

While there is no doubt that southwestern Arkansas proved to be an unsafe and rowdy area during this era of change, it is unfair to suggest that law and order prevailed before Reconstruction. On the contrary, brutality was just as common before as it was after 1865; the difference lay in that black people, who were more often than not the recipients of the brutality, were not treated as victims but property in the antebellum period.

The Republican-led Reconstruction government of Arkansas, while deemed oppressive by many elite white southerners, was actually quite effective. The state spent several thousands of dollars and set aside several sections of land to build free, public schools for both white and black children. In the antebellum years, parents paid subscriptions to schools, which effectively put schooling out of reach for poor whites. Enslaved people were not schooled at all, of course. This had the effect that upward of 50 percent of Arkansas men were deemed illiterate in a Reconstruction-sponsored survey.[196] Free schools, segregated by race, were opened in 1871, 1872 and 1901.[197] The Reconstruction government provided for a public university system as well. The Arkansas Industrial University, which would morph into the University of Arkansas, was funded by the Morrill Land Grant Act of 1862.

The creation of a viable public school system assists in creating strong, sustainable economic growth. Arkansas came late to the game, and for a long time, the Great Bend area lacked access to higher education. That would gradually change, however, as rapid industrialization brought new people and new opportunities to southwestern Arkansas.

The New Labor Force of Southwestern Arkansas

Arkansas' historic link to an agricultural economy did not diminish after the Civil War, but it expanded to include more industrial activities, including timber and mineral mining. These more "northern" efforts brought many new people to southwestern Arkansas but also entrenched the division between the labor and the employer classes.

Sharecropping and tenant farming replaced the plantation system after the Civil War. These farming methods, where farmers did not own their land but rented either in cash or by sharing future crops with the landowners, were simply a continuation of the feudal methods of land use; tenant farming had been prevalent before the Civil War. The tenant and sharecropping systems affected nearly 40 percent of the people living in the counties surrounding the Great Bend of the Red River—Miller, Lafayette, Little River and Hempstead—by 1910.[198] This figure was possibly much higher in the decades immediately following the Civil War, but opportunities in Texarkana and in larger cities siphoned many workers from the countryside into the city. The farmers who remained championed their cause through populist farmers' alliances, where they sought to redress their grievances against high rents, mortgage and railroad shipping rates; unfair competition due to the mechanization of farming; and disparities in income. Their efforts to reform the Arkansas land system did not pay off, however. In 1888, Charles Norwood of Prescott, nominated by the Union Labor Party and strongly supported by both white and black farmers, was defeated by the Democratic candidate, James P. Eagle. Voters in Hempstead, Miller and Lafayette Counties overwhelmingly voted for Norwood. After the close election, supporters of the Democratic Party proposed and passed bills to curtail voting rights, including poll taxes and literacy tests.[199] Others banded with laborers to form the Socialist Party, which became a sizeable minority party in northeast Texas, Oklahoma, Louisiana and Arkansas in the early twentieth century.[200] For example, Bowie County, the entity that encompasses the Texas portion of Texarkana, claimed a 30 percent socialist vote in the 1912 elections.[201] The Southern Tenants Farmers Union (STFU), organized in Tyronza, Arkansas, in the 1930s in response to the perceived wasteful policies of the Agricultural Adjustment Act passed during the Roosevelt's First New Deal, continued the tradition of communal revolt. Composed of both black and whites, the socialist-leaning STFU worked with Methodist ministers to bring economic parity

A family picked cotton in Miller County in this photograph taken after the Civil War. Sharecropping became a way of life in the prairies surrounding the Red River, where cotton remained king. *From the collections of the Arkansas Historical Commission.*

to Arkansas after the complete failure of the sharecropping system but ultimately failed.[202]

After the war, poor whites and free blacks were suddenly on an equal economic footing but stratified socially through mutual stereotypes and social competition. From these lower socioeconomic groups came the majority of the free labor who found work in towns as unskilled workers. Often, "free labor" was a misnomer. After Reconstruction ended, Arkansas imposed the convict lease system, which allowed private contractors to "rent" the labor of men who had been sentenced to prison. Many of these prisoners were simply unemployed people who were caught loitering, some were convicted because they owed debts they could not repay and others were charged with misdemeanor crimes. Leased convicts, both blacks and whites, were set out to work clearing fields, hauling coal and cutting timber. In an investigative article published in the *Arkansas Gazette* in 1888, the conditions of these work camps proved shocking. Law enforcement officers whipped men for failing to meet their daily quota of coal. The lashes caused sores "from the size of a man's finger nail [*sic*] to the size of his hand."[203]

Prior to the Civil War, indigent, free men and women (the latter often widows) bonded themselves to other parties for a period of time to write off their debts. Orphans were apprenticed until they reached maturity. In the era after the Civil War, counties began erecting poorhouses (also called poor farms) to deal with the increasing number of people who could not pay debts incurred by the growing disparities between wages and costs of living. In the Great Bend region, Hempstead County opened a poorhouse in the 1870s, adding an additional building for the insane and disabled in 1902.[204] Poverty proved to become a growing and stubborn reminder of the southern class system. Evidence of pellagra, hookworms and malnourishment increased. An archaeological and anthropological expedition in Lafayette County near the Cedar Grove plantation, for example, unearthed the graves of a family of poor whites who exhibited signs of hunger resulting from a poor diet based mainly on hominy, pork, cornbread and molasses.[205]

After emancipation, whites, blacks and immigrants settled in Texarkana, as railroads beckoned with job opportunities. Black, immigrant and white workers, both skilled and unskilled, who worked for Jay Gould's Missouri Pacific Railroad system attempted to gain better wages and improve working conditions in the system-wide strike of 1886. The strike, organized by the Knights of Labor, reached into the Texarkana yards. For three weeks, commerce halted in the Great Bend region, and citizens not connected to the railroad became angry. The Miller County sheriff asked for the National Guard to stop the strike, which was ultimately unsuccessful.[206] Ashdown, Hope and Lewisville also saw a steady stream of new workers who desired to work in the timber industries, cotton gins or the laying of tracks. The influx of newcomers, coupled with increasing modernization, urbanization and an insistence on the old ways by "old guard" Southern Democrats, led to much racial prejudice and violence. Black men were often suspected of lusting after white women, so perceived "outrages" were dealt with harshly, and often the accused did not have a day in court. In one of the more notorious incidents from the region, a black man named Henry Smith, who was accused of killing a white girl in Paris, Texas, was apprehended at his mother's home in Hope in 1893. He was taken back to Paris, where he faced a horrific lynching that had been advertised over a week before. Over ten thousand people reportedly came to the Texas and Pacific Railway depot south of downtown Paris to watch Henry Smith be slowly roasted and eventually burned to death.[207]

THE RAILROADS COME TO SOUTHWESTERN ARKANSAS

Up until 1875, steamships on the Red River proved to be the most reliable kind of transportation for long-distance travel and freight traffic in southwestern Arkansas, as roads, many still charging tolls, proved cumbersome to navigate. However, the river was not navigable all year, as low water made passage at times impossible. The railroads changed this tradition. In an 1896 promotional book extolling the miracle of rail transport, marketers from the Missouri Pacific Railroad described the scene at Fulton, the epicenter of the Great Bend region: "Here, tied up against the bank, can occasionally be seen the forlorn looking little steam boats, which alone can ascend the river to this point, although before the supremacy of the railroad, the river-carrying trade from Fulton was of considerable importance and the principal means for the shipment of the large cotton crops raised in the Red River bottoms."[208] For the foreseeable future, Fulton would remain an important commercial link in the economy of southwestern Arkansas—only it would do so with the railroads, not necessarily by steamboat.

Railroads began early in Arkansas, but no track was laid in the Great Bend region during the antebellum period. The Mississippi, Ouachita and Red River Railroad, which was to terminate in Fulton, was incorporated in 1852, and the Cairo and Fulton Railroad had been chartered in 1853.[209] A congressional act gave the Cairo and Fulton Railroad eminent domain for over one million acres for construction.[210] Original construction plans approved the gauge for the tracks according to the standard for most southern railroads—five feet, six inches—and much of the track was bought from France. However, underfunding, budget constraints and investment losses hampered the advent of the railroads until after the Civil War—and then it was, no pun intended, full steam ahead.

The Reconstruction government under Powell Clayton assisted in financing the railroads through public bonds and eminent domain. Thus, the Cairo and Fulton Railroad, which was chartered to travel between Cairo, Illinois, and Fulton, Arkansas, was able to build its right of way as the reorganized Cairo, Arkansas and Texas Railroad. It merged with the St. Louis and Iron Mountain Railroad in 1874, thus creating a line that extended from the Red River all the way to St. Louis. The original track gauge had to be changed to accommodate the accepted northern, or standard, gauge of four feet, eight and a half inches. In later years, the railroad would come under the umbrella of Jay Gould's Missouri Pacific Railroad.

The old gives way to new in this photograph of the railroad bridge in Fulton. With the steam trains making overland passage and river crossings much easier, the steamboat that is moored in the background was becoming obsolete. *From the collections of the Arkansas Historical Commission.*

Several major and minor railroads crisscrossed the Great Bend region by the turn of the twentieth century. The St. Louis and Southwestern, also known as the Cotton Belt, came through the Great Bend region in 1879. One of the lines for the St. Louis–San Francisco Railway crossed the Red River at Fulton. A narrow-gauge railroad (three feet gauge) in Hempstead County moved timber, and another narrow-gauge railroad, the Texas and St. Louis Railway, built 340 miles of track through the region in the 1880s.[211]

The Texas and Pacific Railway was one of the most prolific railroads in southwestern Arkansas, as it was originally intended to be a transcontinental line. Before the Civil War, Congress debated whether the transcontinental railroad should take a northern route, from Nebraska westward, or a southern route, from Texas westward. Congress even bought a section of land from Mexico—the Gadsden Purchase—in preparation for election of the southern route. However, when Congress finally got around to voting on the Pacific Railway Act in 1862, the southern states had seceded, and thus the northern route got the nod. After the war, Congress revived the idea of a southern transcontinental line, and the Texas and Pacific Railway received

A locomotive of the Graysonia, Nashville and Ashdown Railroad has a 2-6-0 configuration. *From author's collection.*

In 1883, Washington was still the county seat of Hempstead County, but its days as the center of southwestern Arkansas were over. With the arrival of the railroads, Hope and Texarkana surpassed it in prominence. *From the collections of the Arkansas Historical Commission.*

a federal charter to construct a route from Texas to California. Funding problems and construction delays hampered the effort, however, and the actual route was not completed until the 1880s.

The new railroads did not benefit everyone, however. Many of the older settlements in the Great Bend region were bypassed by the railroads either immediately or gradually as new towns were built to accommodate the new economy.

TEXARKANA: TOE THE LINE

In December 1873, the Texas and Pacific Railway reached the Arkansas border, where it met with the tracks of the Cairo and Fulton Railroad in January of the next year. This junction gave birth to the city of Texarkana. "Why should Texarcana [*sic*]," an editorial in the *Arkansas Gazette* mused one year prior, "a mere point in the woods, beside a blazed pine, on a bleak and desolate ridge, with not even good water to recommend it, be made the great meeting point of railroads to the northeast and southwest?"[212]

The question had some merit. Several thriving and established cities already dotted the region, so there did not seem to be a real need to found Texarkana. The location of the junction, however, spelled out the future for the town. Sitting on the line between Texas and Arkansas, the new city was twelve miles south of one of the earliest river fords, White Oak Shoals. This ford would become the best location for a railroad bridge, as it had bedrock underneath. Just west of the shoals sat Laynesport, head of navigation for the Red River and a perfect outlet for all the freight and passengers the railroad would bring. A few miles to the northeast lay Fulton, the thriving steamboat port and a true "Gateway to the Southwest." Louisiana, with its cotton fields and as-yet discovered oil deposits, beckoned about twenty miles to the southeast. Texarkana sat in the right place: flat prairie land conducive to building right of ways, far enough away from the river to avoid floods and direct lines to other transportation centers. Soon, Texarkana's railroads would usurp all the other methods of conveyances, and the center of the Great Bend region would shift from Washington and Fulton to the twin city.

The junction and the building of Texarkana took place along the Index Line, which was appropriately named State Line Avenue. Established by the Adams-Onis Treaty of 1819 and subsequently surveyed by the Mexican and American governments in 1832, the arbitrary line—it did not align with any

The bridge over the Red River between Texarkana and Ashdown marked the Index Line between Texas and Arkansas. Part of the bridge could be drawn up to allow steamships to pass as they made their way toward Laynesport. *From the collections of the Arkansas Historical Commission.*

By the late 1870s, Texarkana had become a boomtown. A well stood in the middle of what would become State Line Avenue. *From the collections of the Arkansas Historical Commission.*

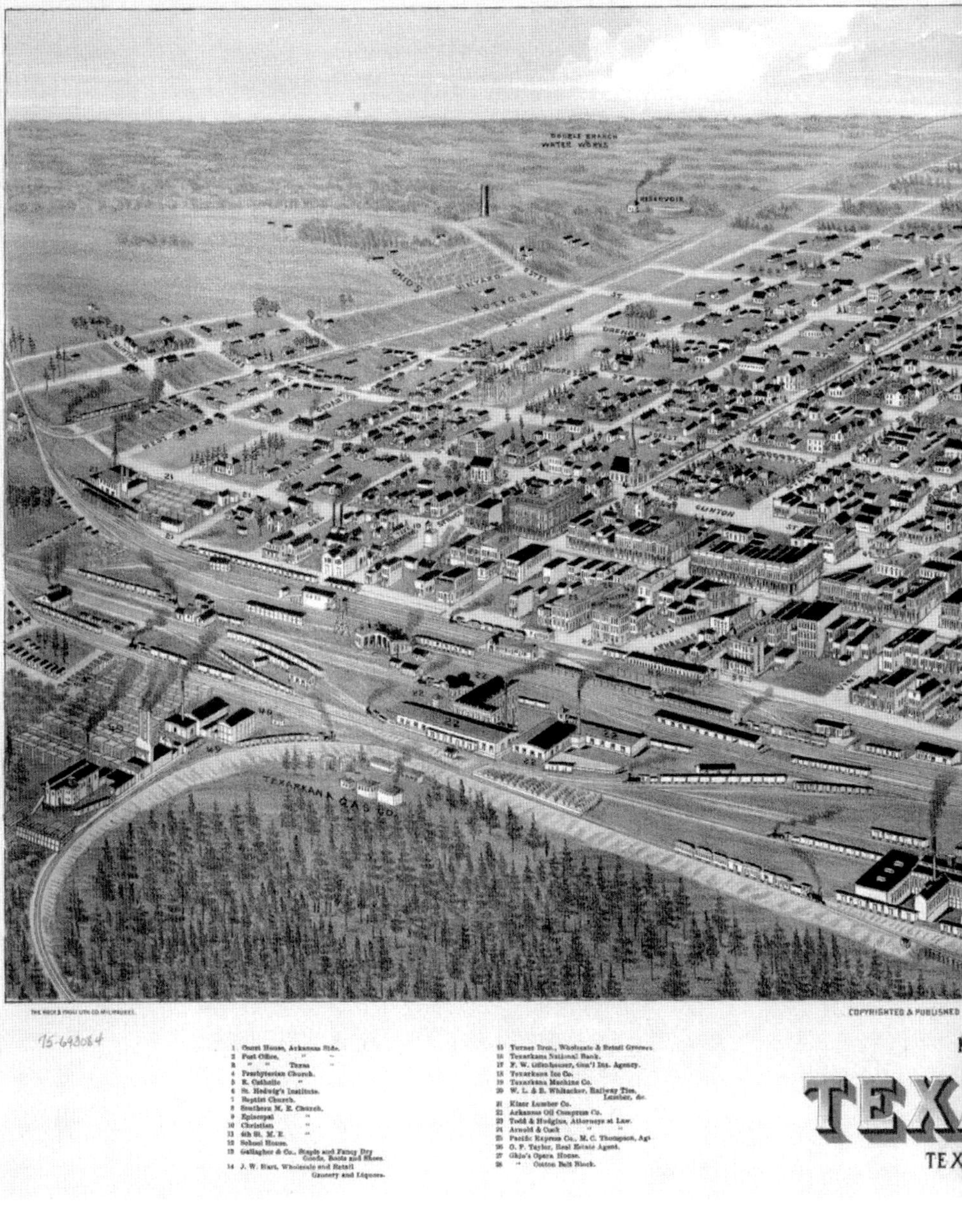

A bird's-eye view of Texarkana shows how much the city had grown by 1888. *Courtesy Library of Congress.*

BROAD
ST.
WALNUT
LAUREL
ASH
BEECH
PECAN
RYCKORT
LOCUST
SECOND ST MILWAUKEE WIS.
OF.
KANA,
NSAS.
Smith & Arbuckle, Real Estate Agents
Henry & Henry, Attorneys at Law.
L. A. Byrne, Attorney at Law.
The Andrews Block.
Scott & Jones, Attorneys at Law.
Cosmopolitan Hotel,
W. H. McCartney, Prop.
First National Bank.
Union Depot, W. Williams, Agent.
Gate City Lumber Co.
Frank G. Miller, Texarkana Iron Works.
W. E. Varner's Brick Yard.
Thos. Hale & Co., Druggists.
Division of Maps
Library of Congress

natural landmarks—was ratified in 1838. As a result, Old Miller County was dissolved and absorbed by Hempstead and Lafayette Counties. But the county reappeared in 1874 with the advent of the railroads. Much smaller than it had been in its first incarnation, the new Miller County came about when Lafayette County gave up its western portion past the Red River. Texarkana was selected as the county seat. Rondo, at one time the main settlement of the area, lost its post office in favor of the burgeoning city of Texarkana in 1893, the same year that the St. Louis and Iron Mountain Railroad donated land for the construction of the Miller County Courthouse.[213] Texarkana also served as the county seat for Bowie County, Texas, after a successful campaign by its citizens to replace the 1841 seat, Boston. In 1891, the courthouse in Texarkana burned, and the county seat reverted to what was now called New Boston (residents of Boston moved north to reach the Texas and Pacific Railway line and named the settlement New Boston). Texarkana, Texas, continued to campaign to become the county's capital, but a final 1926 vote determined that the courthouse was to remain in New Boston.[214]

Railroads defined the city. So many came into the hub and were rechartered, renamed, consolidated, bankrupted or sold that complete lists are hard to conjure. A partial inventory would include:[215] the Cairo and Fulton Railroad; the Texas and Pacific Railway; the St. Louis, Iron Mountain and Southern Railroad; the St. Louis–Southwestern Railway; the St. Louis and Southwestern Railroad of Texas (this would become known as the Cotton Belt); the Kansas City Southern Railway; the Texarkana and Fort Smith Railway (previously known as the Texarkana and Northern Railway); the Texarkana, Shreveport and Natchez Railway; the Memphis, Dallas and Gulf Railway; and the Missouri Pacific Railroad, which consolidated many lines under its robber baron founder, Jay Gould. Narrow-gauge (three feet) railroads also came through town, such as the Texas and St. Louis Railway (later chartered under the St. Louis, Arkansas and Texas Railway), mostly to haul timber and cotton from rural areas.[216]

The many tracks that came through Texarkana created havoc with its city planning. A newspaper jokingly described grade crossings at Texarkana in a 1926 editorial, which extolled that the Kansas City Southern tracks that met with West Seventh Street could carry a hapless accident victim's "remains as far as the casket factory. Properly provided there, it is only a few yards on down the track to the sulphur factory."[217]

Today, railroad companies still maintain regional hubs in Texarkana, including the Kansas City Southern Railway, the Union Pacific Railroad, Amtrak's Texas Eagle, the Arkansas Southern Railroad, the DeQueen and

Above: Texarkana remained true to its southern roots as it became an important cotton-shipping center. *From author's collection.*

Left: The Miller County courthouse—with Texarkana, Arkansas, as the county seat—was erected on land donated by the St. Louis, Iron Mountain and Southern Railway. *From author's collection.*

Eastern Railroad, the Kiamichi Railroad, the Louisiana and North West Railroad, the Prescott and Northwestern Railroad, the Texas and Northern Railway and the Texas Northeastern Railroad.[218]

The Cairo and Fulton Railroad surveyed and sold the first plats of real estate on the Arkansas side of State Line Avenue, with the Texas and Pacific doing the same on the western side. The early streets paralleled the railroad tracks and thus were not carved on the simple cardinal axis of the Index Line, thus providing the city's center with a crooked alignment and quirky architecture. "Some office buildings are wedge-shaped, and others have walls staggered or even slightly zigzagged to fit available ground space," described the *WPA Guide to Arkansas*. "Roofs have also been chopped into odd angles, with curious gables and diminutive towers springing up here and there."[219] The earliest settlements sat on the Texas side, but a letter writer to the *Arkansas Gazette* praised the virtue of both halves of the city, calling the region "the richest cotton country in the world, best pine timber, purest of water" with a "choice to settle in Arkansas and Texas."[220] People came from all over to settle the new town; some left area villages to find work, while others relocated from distant states or countries to take advantage of the city's possibilities. Some of the early immigrants included the family of Scott Joplin, a musician who introduced the world to ragtime music. He learned to perfect his natural talent for piano playing in Texarkana, where he took lessons from Julian Weiss, a German-born musician. Joplin grew to become an icon of American music. He wrote "The Maple Leaf Rag" and "The Entertainer" and penned two operas: *Guest of Honor* and *Tremonisha*.

Texarkana centered on two buildings: the federal courthouse, which was built from Texas granite and Arkansas limestone, bisected by the state line; and Union Station, where both passengers and mail waited for trains on either the Arkansas or Texas sides. The depot occupied almost an entire city block. The whites-only waiting room was separated by the state line, and each side had blacks-only waiting rooms to comply with the Jim Crow laws of both Texas and Arkansas.[221]

Schooling came to Texarkana's youth in a haphazard fashion. The postwar constitutions of both states stipulated that publicly funded schools should be erected by municipalities or school districts and provided free to both white and black children. In Texarkana, the first publicly funded schools were not erected until the 1880s and became standard by the turn of the century.[222] Until then, white children relied on private, subscription-based schools, and black children received education at Freedmen schools or in churches. Some schools, such as the one constructed in 1925 at

Texarkana's Union Depot took up several city blocks and marked the southern end of State Line Avenue. The depot was demolished in the 1920s to make way for a more modern terminal. *From author's collection.*

Modern Union Station's architecture is reminiscent of the grand concourses at New York and Chicago. Sadly, both the station and Hotel McCartney suffer from neglect today, though Amtrak makes daily stops. *From author's collection.*

State Line Avenue, as viewed from Union Station, cuts directly through the federal post office and courthouse building. The building on the left houses the Museum of Regional History. *From author's collection.*

the corner of Pinehurst and Preston Streets, was partially funded by the Rosenwald Foundation.[223] As the new center of the region, Texarkana also became the center of education. Texarkana College, an outgrowth of the Texarkana, Texas school system, opened its doors in 1927. East Texas State University opened a branch in Texarkana in 1971 and became part of the Texas A&M University system in 1996.

Though Texarkana was one city, its geographic location posed unique governmental challenges. At first, trains on the two earliest railroads had to stop and reconfigure cargo, cars and passengers to continue traveling into the next state, as each required different regulations. The Arkansas side sold beer, spirits and liquor, but the Texas side did not. Before interstate compacts between law enforcement agencies, people wanted in one state simply had to cross the line into the other to delay capture.[224] This may have been why one of the major murder sprees in the modern era was never solved. In 1946, five people were killed, with two women sexually tortured before their deaths, in gruesome attacks around Texarkana. Panic swept through Texarkana as local residents, police and even the Texas Rangers descended on the city to investigate what the *Texarkana Gazette* had dubbed the "Phantom Killer." Though the law fingered a suspect, car thief Youell Sweeney, prosecutors were unable to charge him with the homicides because his wife, who had earlier spoken to police about unpublished details of the murders, refused to testify against him in court. The five murders and three assaults that were linked to the Phantom Killer were never solved.[225]

HOPE: WATERMELONS AND MORE

The bypassing of Washington by the Cairo and Fulton Railroad in 1874 did not immediately signal the end of the Hempstead County's seat—the town actually erected a new courthouse in 1874—but gradually Hope, a new city established on the railroad right of way, would usurp its importance. Hope became the county seat in 1938, after much contentious debate and three previous attempts. By then, it had already become the county's commercial center.

In 1873, the first town lots surrounding the wooden depot in this burgeoning city were laid out and sold by the Cairo and Fulton Railroad, which ran the first locomotive called the "Roswell Beebe" into town in 1873.[226] The town's charter in 1875 brought public schools, hotels, cotton gins, timber yards, sawmills, brick making, a broom handle factory, a wagon factory and a steel bridge manufacturing facility to the area, all aiding in the town's economic success.[227] In the 1940s, Hope residents supported the creation of the Southwest Proving Grounds, a federal defense project erected to prepare for the oncoming war. The site selected for the grounds was in northeastern Hempstead County, at the former town site of Marlbrook, the oldest settlement in the county. Over 2,500 sharecroppers, tenant farmers and landowners were evicted from the land. The removal of civilian habitation was so complete that even cemeteries were relocated. While the working class found better employment in the construction of the training ground, landowners mourned the loss of their family farms and the paltry compensation they received.[228] Hope's focus on the future served it well, and four specific things and people brought the town fame: education, former Arkansas governor Michael Huckabee, former governor of Arkansas and president of the United States William Jefferson Clinton and watermelons.

From 1895 to 1935, Hope hosted a black teacher college at the Shover Street School, founded by Henry Clay Yerger. This important training ground was one of only three in Arkansas designed for black educators during the period of school segregation and the first to be erected west of the Mississippi River.[229] In 1966, the Red River Vocational and Technical School opened its doors to area students. To better serve the growing, information-

The Missouri Pacific depot at Hope welcomes passengers on Amtrak and sees several freight trains pass through daily. *From the collections of the Arkansas Historical Commission.*

Farms surrounding Hope have a reputation for producing monstrous watermelons. This gargantuan specimen epitomizes the sizes to which the fruits can grow. *From author's collection.*

Not every watermelon in Hope is of disproportionate size; most are grown to eat, not to brag. During the summer, watermelons are sold everywhere. *From the collections of the Arkansas Historical Commission.*

based economy, the school expanded into a community college, governed under the University of Arkansas system.

Two politicians made their marks on the town. Michael Huckabee, a Baptist minister who was born in Hope, was elected governor of the state twice. He distinguished himself by being a progressive, community-minded leader as well as one of only three Republicans to have held the office by that time. William Jefferson Clinton, born in Hope but raised in Hot Springs, became one of the twentieth century's leading politicians. After two non-consecutive terms as state governor, Clinton won the presidential election of 1992 and sat for two terms in office. Though he faced impeachment in his second term, Clinton's policies led to great economic growth in the 1990s, including budget surpluses and deficit eliminations.[230] Clinton's success harks to the state's progressive bent. While southern dogma has reared its head in

The Black Giants, a brass band from Hope, pose for the newspaper photographer in 1912. *From the collections of the Arkansas Historical Commission.*

The Carson and Barnes Circus wintered in Hope. Animal trainer Martha Moore feeds one of the circus's hippos. *From the collections of the Arkansas Historical Commission.*

Arkansan politics many times over the years, it is often tempered by forward-thinking communities and individuals.

Hempstead County has always been known for its capacity to yield delicious fruit. In his memoir, Sam Williams commented that Judge Hubbard's garden patch produced "the finest watermelons" in 1852.[231] The St. Louis and Iron Mountain Railroad even set up a model farm near Hope in the 1890s to encourage farmers to grow fruit trees, in the hopes of increasing freight traffic.[232] This may be why Hope has become known as the watermelon capital of the world.[233] According to local lore, a watermelon seed salesman staged a competition between melon growers in Hempstead County, where farmers were able to grow huge fruits using a new kind of seed. Watermelons that weighed over one hundred pounds became routine contenders. As word about the monstrous fruits spread, city officials latched onto the idea of staging a watermelon festival, complete with competitions, eating contests, pageants and parades. The first festival occurred in 1926. Drought ended the events after four years, but citizens revived the Watermelon Festival in 1976. Many of the watermelons featured in the festival have become state, national and even world record champions.[234]

ASHDOWN: TIMBERLAND

Ashdown, founded in 1892, was not the first contender for the county seat of Little River County, which itself is a newcomer to southwestern Arkansas. Carved from Sevier County in 1867, Little River County's development mirrors that of Hempstead, Miller and Lafayette: many early, antebellum settlements and commercial centers have given way to the modern towns founded along railroad right of ways.

Sevier County was busy and prosperous, but it was also deemed too large for its citizens, as the county seat was situated north of the Little River—the state thus created a new county. Early commerce in the area that became Little River County centered on the Red River, which is now its southern boundary; the Little River, the county's northern boundary; and the military road that reached to Fort Towson in Indian Territory. The Choctaw Nation of Oklahoma now forms the county's western border. Laynesport and Cook's Landing hosted steamboats on the Red River from 1840 to 1890.[235] River crossings could be made at Allen's Ferry, north of Fulton on the Little River; at White Oak Shoals, where the Index Line marked the boundaries

The cottonseed oil mill in Ashdown was one of several employers in the growing seat of Little River County. *From the collections of the Arkansas Historical Commission.*

between Texas and Arkansas; and at Joyner's Ferry across the Red River. The county's oldest settlements no longer exist: Pine Prairie, which centered on the Scott Plantation and a sorghum mill, experienced many floods, and Wallace, an 1850 settlement sponsored by a Dutch merchant, is now just a small collection of houses.

Alleene, a small settlement in the western part of the county, served as Little River County's first seat for approximately one year. Court was held in a simple dogtrot cabin. Rocky Comfort, an antebellum settlement that boasted the first steam-powered cotton gin, became the next capital.[236] Rocky Comfort is now a ghost town, however. When the Arkansas and Choctaw Railroad laid its tracks one mile to the north of town at the turn of the twentieth century, citizens moved closer to commerce and formed Foreman, which is now the second-largest city in Little River County. By 1880, the citizens of Richmond had built a courthouse, and the seat moved there. Founded in the 1850s by settlers from Alabama, Richmond became quite a busy trading center in the antebellum years, with a hotel, banks, several general stores and a coeducational academy tending to the educational needs of white children. Its fate was ultimately sealed, however, when the Texarkana and Fort Smith Railroad laid its tracks away from Richmond. Ashdown, the town that grew up around the tracks, was selected as the final county seat after contentious elections in which Richmonders desperately tried to cling to their status as county seat.

Timber proved to be Ashland's main commercial attraction. Sawmills, gins, woodworks and railroad tie manufacturers counted among the many businesses that spurred growth in Ashdown at the turn of the century. Ultimately, three railroads served Ashdown: the aforementioned Texarkana and Fort Smith Railway (later, the Kansas City Southern); the Memphis, Paris and Gulf Railroad (later, the Graysonia, Nashville and Ashdown Railroad); and the St. Louis–San Francisco Railway.[237] Ashdown continued to grow into Little River County's population center. Several churches, civic organizations and public schools helped the community to grow, but it was not always easy. Southern racial attitudes persisted as whites and blacks competed for work in the mills. Like in most cities, progress can be measured by the investment in education. In Ashdown's earliest attempts at schooling, white children attended class inside a private building; the first black school was built using Rosenwald Foundation funds. In the 1990s, Cossatot Technical College, based in DeQueen, built a satellite campus in Ashdown. The college came under the umbrella of the University of Arkansas system in 1999.[238]

LEWISVILLE: NEW OLD TOWN

Unlike Hempstead, Little River and Miller Counties, Lafayette County maintained its ties to the past by keeping its county seat relatively stable in the period after the Civil War. Lewisville had been declared the county seat already by 1841.[239] However, the St. Louis and Southwestern Railroad (known as the Cotton Belt) and the Louisiana and Arkansas Railroad laid tracks one mile south of Lewisville because farmers and landowners of "Old Lewisville" could not agree on prices for the proposed right of way. The new town, platted by the Southwestern Improvement Association, the town-building branch of the Cotton Belt Railroad, was deemed "New Lewisville," and citizens simply moved their businesses and homes to the new center.[240] "New Lewisville" became "Lewisville" after incorporation in 1889.[241]

The depot, a wooden structure built in 1882 on Spruce Street, became the hub of the new town.[242] Most of the businesses, such as the drugstore and general store, were owned by the Lester family, and residents jokingly contemplated renaming the town "Lesterville."[243] Lewisville's economy centered on cotton; consequently, the earliest land users were large plantations, and the majority of the county's inhabitants were blacks. Lafayette County voted overwhelmingly in favor of secession, and many Civil War regiments were mustered in the county. After the war, tenant farmers and sharecroppers became the county's economic mainstay.[244] Nearby Garland City served as a steamboat stop and ferry landing. Instead of Lewisville, the town of Stamps, which lies to the east, has become the commercial center of the county. Founded as a railroad stop for the Cotton Belt, Stamps grew because of the timber industry. It was also the childhood home of famed poet Maya Angelou.

Lewisville retained the feeling of a country outpost, and due to its reliance on cotton crops, the town's residents had difficulty weathering economic downturns, including the boll weevil epidemic of the 1920s and the Great Depression of the 1930s. The invention by John Rust of the mechanical cotton picker in the 1930s changed the agrarian economy as well, as new, efficient methods threw sharecroppers and tenant farmers off the land. Many farmers abandoned cotton farming and turned to soybeans, corn or wheat; started grazing cattle; or leased their land to timber companies. Tenant farmers and sharecroppers found work in nearby towns. Though by southwestern Arkansas' standards the longest-serving of county seats, Lewisville has the youngest courthouse: it was built in 1942 by the Public Works Administration, replacing two earlier ones.[245] On the courthouse lawn sits the Steel family cemetery, which existed before New Lewisville was platted and therefore became part of the courthouse survey. The graves of county judge John Steel; his wife, Elizabeth; their son, Confederate lieutenant Egbert B. Steel of the First Arkansas Cavalry; his wife, Eugenia; and son Lewis now find their resting place in the shadow of the courthouse.[246]

Lafayette County experienced an oil boom in the 1920s and 1930s, and several fields in Garland City, Bradley, Lewisville and McKamie were explored. While the amount of crude proved to be sufficient, bad conservation and management efforts yielded only a fraction of the estimated $37 million worth of oil. Exploration still continues, but much of the oil economy has moved farther south into Louisiana.[247]

The "New South" that emerged after the Civil War changed southwestern Arkansas in many ways. Not only did it effect how inhabitants conducted

The building that housed Lester's Drug Store in Lewisville is now a registered historic building. In this photograph from the 1930s, men visit with one another outside of the store. *From the collections of the Arkansas Historical Commission.*

commerce, but it also led to new realities in terms of race, geography and cultural direction. As the United States began to homogenize into one large unit after the country moved from sectional differences to global concerns, the regional character of southwestern Arkansas gave way to a more nationalized one. When the modern era arrived in the Great Bend region, southwestern Arkansans, like all Americans, adjusted to a wider world.

Chapter 4

Along the Bankhead Highway

The Modern Era

In 1941, the federal government published *Arkansas: A Guide to the State*. A comprehensive volume that described the culture, commerce and cities of Arkansas, the guide also gave touring information for many federal highways that crossed the state after a series of legislative acts in the 1920s created a national road system. The route of U.S. 67, which in places paralleled the Southwestern Trail of the Great Bend region, stood out for what it did not include. Washington, center of the region for over 120 years at that point—and, at one time, the state's capital, Hempstead County seat and commercial center—had been bypassed by the highway altogether.

"Right from Hope on State 4, graveled," the guide informed, "to Washington, 10.2 m. (372 alt., 432 pop.), one of the most highly civilized communities in early Arkansas, State capital in 1863–1865, and now a living museum of old houses, old trees, and old memories."[248] Offering a very detailed history of the town, the guide described what artifacts remained:

> *The Old Chihuahua Trail* [Southwestern Trail] *ran down Franklin Avenue, still the main street of Washington. At the junction of Franklin and State 4 is Washington Tavern or Traveler's Inn, built in 1830. The inn is a two-story building, constructed mostly of hand-hewn timber that was later weatherboarded…the Old Baptist Church, built around 1830 and still in use, is a small frame building with a pediment supported by four columns. Three of these are the original hewn cypress trunks; the fourth is a box column replacing one that was cut up for firewood during the War*

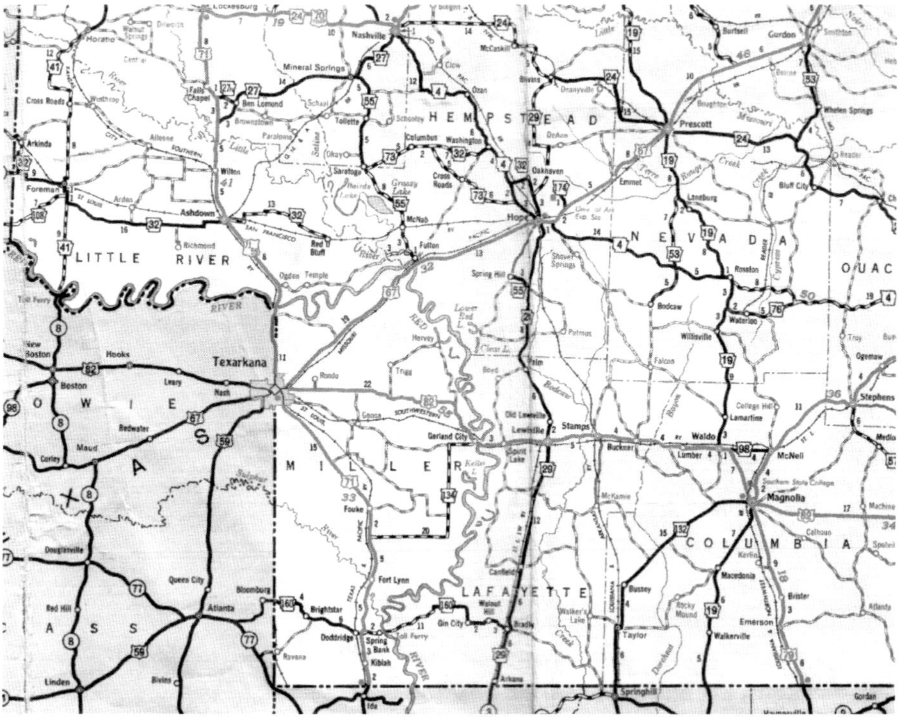

By the early 1950s, traffic had moved away from the antebellum centers to follow the path of the railroads, and the Bankhead Highway had become US 67. *From author's collection.*

> *Between the States when the church was used as a hospital. The one-story frame A.O. Stuart House, built of hand-finished lumber in 1852–1857, is still in a fair state of repair.*[249]

Washington, once the heart of southwestern Arkansas and one of the busiest cities in the history of the state, had become a roadside relic of the automobile age.

Reactionary Politics and Progressive Reforms

At the turn of the twentieth century, southwestern Arkansas was booming. Railroads flowed in and out of Texarkana, Hope, Lewisville and Ashdown; abundant timber fed sawmills and furniture manufacturing facilities; and cotton was king. It seemed as though the Great Bend region was turning its back on its agrarian past and joining the future as an industrial center. This quick change, however, resulted in clashes between the "Old South" and the "New South." The incidences of racial violence, coupled with the modern march toward reform and civil rights, were in no way unique to the region; in fact, they mirrored the growing pains of all of the western states emerging from Reconstruction.

The insistence of the former economic elites that they had the right to mete justice as they deemed fit harked back to the period of southern white hegemony and manifested itself through Jim Crow laws and extra-legal violence in the modern era. As African Americans gained economic independence and flooded into towns in search of new opportunities, they discovered that old prejudices followed them. An ordinance in Texarkana, passed in 1891, barred African Americans from enjoying the city's only public park, and blacks in Lewisville felt "the hand of oppression."[250] In Rocky Comfort, the murder of prominent landowner James Stockton was avenged when a mob of "several hundred" white men and "Stockton's negroes came for a necktie party," hanging the accused killer, an African American man named General Ducket, on a "nice leaning willow tree." Ducket's friends, Ed Gooden and Joe King, were also hanged.[251] In 1922, Harley Owen, accused of murdering a Texarkana policeman, was shot and killed in front of a mob of several thousand after he was chased into a town park.[252] Charles Powell of Lewisville, who allegedly killed a deputy sheriff, was hanged by a mob of 150 people.[253] In Hope, Browning Tuggle was hanged from a scaffold attached to the city's water tower in front of a large crowd after having been accused of raping a white woman and taken from the county jail with "no interference." Tuggle's body "was riddled with bullets, the shots being fired by infuriated members of the mob" and left hanging all night as a warning to the city's black population. Fearing a riot, 250 special deputies patrolled the city for two days to keep the peace.[254] The crimes that the African American men were accused of may or may not have been committed; the problem with vigilante justice was that the accused usually did not have their day in court or were given quick show trials, and thus innocence or guilt were never proven.

The Ku Klux Klan, which dissolved during military reconstruction, reemerged in southwestern Arkansas by the turn of the twentieth century as a moralistic, anti-Catholic, anti-Semitic, nativist and racist organization. The Klan, which changed from its original purpose of outright voter intimidation and racial control to a "secret society" with a political message of reactionary conservatism, was not necessarily responsible for lynchings, although mob members who meted out vigilante justice may have been

Texarkana grew into a major commercial center by the twentieth century. *From author's collection.*

Before the mall and Interstate 30 diverted traffic away from downtown, Broad Street in Texarkana was a great place to shop. *From the collections of the Texas/Dallas History and Archives Division, Dallas Public Library.*

supporters. The majority of Klan members, who tended to be leading citizens such as doctors, lawyers, planters and bankers, claimed responsibility for public floggings of those they deemed undesirable. For example, the Klan beat a bootlegger and dumped him onto a street in downtown Hope; in Texarkana, a young black man was kidnapped and whipped with a wet rope for allegedly "fooling around with a white woman" in 1922. Members of the Klan also burned gambling halls, saloons and brothels.[255]

Interestingly, the extreme methods used by people who felt they had to maintain their self-proclaimed domination were juxtaposed by progressive attempts at reform during the same period. The progressives believed government involvement, not vigilantism, proved the best way to induce moralistic change and were much more successful in getting their points across. For example, the movement to ban the sale of alcohol became an important political platform for both conservatives and progressives in the early twentieth century. Several temperance organizations existed in southwestern Arkansas and were successful in getting laws passed that made the acquisition of a license to sell liquor difficult. Prison reform proved to be another progressive success. The convict lease system, which existed prior to the Civil War, had become even more abusive during the Reconstruction era. Populists in the Union Labor Party, Agricultural Wheel, Famers Alliances and the Knights of Labor championed the idea that instead of leasing prisoners to private individuals or businesses that might lead to abuse, they should work for the state in road building crews. The plan allowed for prisoners to earn money to use toward paying fines and fees, in addition to accumulating a small amount of savings upon release. Progressives also believed that the labor would make convicted men feel better about themselves, as they learned a job they could perform after their sentence was over and they realized they were helping others.[256] Eugene Lankford, an Arkansas judge, echoed the idea when he wrote that "a prison that does not turn a prisoner out a better person than when he entered it has failed its chief purpose."[257] Governor George Donaghey approved of the plan, and public road building replaced private plantation work for convicts—just in time for the federal and statewide push to build "good roads."

THE OPEN ROAD BECKONS

The earliest trails used by Native Americans, and then emigrants, in southwestern Arkansas never exhibited the best quality. Muddy and choked by underbrush, often they proved impassable, and even after the military roads and postal routes had been constructed, they did not necessarily induce ardor. Sam Williams did not have kind things to say about the roads surrounding Fulton in the winter of 1850: "The roads…which in the region around Fulton were never noted for their excellence, were placed in a horrid condition. That notorious piece of road known as the 'pine flats,' laying between Fulton and Bridge Creek, famed far and wide as the worst bit of road in the entire Southwest, was absolutely impassable."[258] As time passed, roads continued to be maintained in a haphazard fashion. Travelers would often find the southwestern trails littered with rocks, stumps and fallen trees; instead of removing obstructions, thcy would simply circumvent them, thus creating new trails that themselves could become mired messes.[259]

The quest to build better roads for improved travel began in 1891 in Boston through the League of American Wheelmen. Its purpose was to lobby and promote roads conducive to bicycling, which had become a national craze after the safety bicycle replaced the suicidal penny-farthing. Lewisville had its own bicycle club that sought road improvements in 1896.[260] However, soon the automobile eclipsed bicycles as the preferred method of personal transportation, as enthusiastic men and women embraced the idea of touring, and what would become known as the "Good Roads Movement" shifted from advocating bike trails to building auto trails.

The very first auto trails were patched together by a series of maintained roadbeds funded privately, but that proved insufficient. Although there were a few farmers who needed convincing that the automobile was not just some kind of rich man's fad, the need for reliable roads gained popular support quite early in Arkansas. Prescient community leaders realized that the state, which boasted many scenic destinations like Hot Springs and the Ozark mountain range, could benefit from tourism very well. "The Ozarks will then become the playground of America," an editorial in *Arkansas Highways* maintained.[261] Thus, the Good Roads League of the State of Arkansas formed in 1896 during a convention in Little Rock. There, Governor James Clark declared February 25 to be "Good Roads Day."[262] Soon, several state and federal acts were passed that facilitated road building. In the beginning, Arkansas roads were funded by auto registration fees; later, gasoline was taxed to add more funding monies. Men who did not want to pay the tax—or could not afford to—had to commit to working one week out of the year in building roads, and much prison labor was used to build new trails.[263]

By the late teens, road building had become a new, important governmental function. Vehicle registrations increased in Arkansas from 3,596 in 1913 to

The Bankhead Highway brought businessmen and tourists to southwestern Arkansas, and many roadside motels catered to them, like this one in Fulton. *From author's collection.*

over 60,000 in 1920, and the necessity of having good roads became readily apparent.[264] The Federal Aid Act of 1916 provided funds to assist states in building new—or expanding existing—postal roads. In 1923, when the United States government withheld funds because Arkansas roads were still sub-par, the state passed the Harrelson Road Law, which created the highway commission and the first official state highway system. These state highways were given sequential numbers in 1925 through the U.S. Bureau of Public Roads.[265] In southwestern Arkansas, three state highways connected the region with the wider world; they were designated as routes 67, 71 and 82.

The Bankhead Highway, also known as the "Broadway of America," became Route 67. Reaching from Washington, D.C., to San Diego, it paralleled the military road from Little Rock to Fulton, running along the pine ridge line that cut a diagonal path through Arkansas. However, this new road diverted from the older trail in that it connected with cities situated on railroad right of ways, thus bypassing the older towns. Named after Senator John H. Bankhead from Alabama, who was president of the U.S. Good Roads Association, the Bankhead Highway/Route 67 traversed through Prescott, Hope, Fulton and Texarkana before entering Texas. In Hope, the highway entered town as East Third Street, which the city paved in 1926.[266] At Fulton, the highway had to cross the Red River. Early travelers

Once again, a photo from Fulton shows the wave of the future: a bus on U.S. 67 passes over the railroad tracks, signifying the road's replacement of rail travel. *From the collections of the Arkansas Historical Commission.*

waited at the banks for the ferry to assist them, but in 1925, the highway commission proposed building a toll bridge "that will be a big boost for the whole county, and it will pay for itself in a year or two."[267] State legislators then hatched a plan to borrow money for the bridge construction instead of receiving money from a bond election.[268] This new scheme, the first in the state, proved to be controversial—apparently, a group of investors believed it had received from the state the right to build a private toll bridge at Fulton and sued to recoup its investment. The state prevailed, and the toll bridge at Fulton was in operation by 1929.[269] In 1927, Arkansas declared eminent domain on all toll bridges, including the toll bridge operating on Highway 82 at Garland City.[270]

Route 71 journeyed from Fort Smith to Ashdown and Texarkana through the breathtaking scenery of the Ouachita Mountains and the Arkansas National Forest. Because of its tourism appeal, the highway became one of the first roads to be paved in southwestern Arkansas. The highway department used burned shale, a byproduct of coal mining, to make the street durable and weather-ready.[271] The road's success in bringing automobile tourists led the National Forest Service to carve the Ouachita National Forest from the

Arkansas National Forest in 1926.[272] In Texarkana, Route 71 became State Line Avenue and followed the surveyed Index Line to the Red River. In the 1920s, a drawbridge was erected across the Red River to accommodate gravel barges that still plied the river, which were low enough to clear the bridge without needing the draw accommodation.[273] The erection of a drawbridge may have indicated a desire to resurrect inland water transportation.

Route 82, which runs from Georgia to New Mexico, was designated a federal highway in 1932, connecting several regional roads in a straight line through the south-central United States. In the Great Bend region, the highway connects Texarkana, Garland City and Lewisville. Early on, however, Lafayette County lagged behind other counties in road improvements. By 1926, only 56.7 miles of road had been paved in the county, compared to 150.0 miles in Hempstead County;[274] this may have been due to the spongy soil surrounding the Red River, which made construction difficult. A steel-truss bridge was erected over the Red River in Garland City in 1931, but before it opened, a still-unknown assailant blew it up. Once repaired, the bridge supplanted the ferry and charged tolls until Arkansas made all of its bridges free. The bridge has since been razed.

The new highways brought many tourists to the area. Though they did not tend to make the Great Bend their destination, they nonetheless needed overnight accommodations, and roadside tourist courts, full-service gas stations, restaurants and free camping grounds hugged the thoroughfares to cater to them. More often than not, the modern conveniences pushed the smaller, simpler hotels out of business. The hotels in Lewisville, which relied on the railroads to bring guests, closed their doors once Route 82 was able to take travelers from Mississippi to Texarkana in one day. Another casualty of the automobile age was the hotel on Spirit Lake near Garland City. Operated by "a one-armed Irish man, Mr. Harnegan," the hotel could be reached only by an excursion boat that ferried passengers after they disembarked from the train, which stopped at the lake for several hours to replenish its water supply. The hotel featured a restaurant, serene views and, rumor had it, a gambling den. The hotel burned in the 1930s and was never rebuilt.[275]

Not everyone was thrilled with the influx of tourists in the region. In what may have been a satirical take on the old folktale of the Arkansas Traveler—in which a visitor to Arkansas is never given a straight answer to his questions—some citizens in southwestern Arkansas gave tourists a literal runaround. *Arkansas Highways* noted in an editorial in 1925 that "it has taken several days [for tourists] to make the trip from Hot Springs to Texarkana. Investigation in each case reveals that the tourists have been routed wrong."

Tourists who left Hot Springs and entered Hempstead County asked for directions and apparently were routed into a muddied wilderness where they had to be pulled from soggy back roads, for a fee. The Good Roads Movement was not amused.[276]

The United States authorized the building of massive thoroughfares to link major cities in the Federal Aid Act of 1956. Built on the recommendation of General Jack Pershing, who as commander of the U.S. forces in World War I witnessed numerous obstacles to overland troop and machine transport, these super highways proved to be fast and efficient. Completed in 1968, the path of Interstate 30 mimicked that of Route 67.[277] While convenient, the interstate system led to faster travel, standardized expectations and the loss of a sense of place. The road siphoned visitors from the city centers of Texarkana and Hope and paid very little attention to the Red River as it passed by Fulton.

Hanging On

The Red River has flooded countless times over its million-year history, and at least four disastrous floods have been noted in its recorded history, not counting the many times the river leapt over its banks before the Great Raft was permanently cleared. In the winter of 1843, the river swelled so rapidly that residents were caught in their beds, unaware, and steamboats came to rescue people who had sought refuge in trees. In 1844, during "one of her periodic booms, she kept on a-booming." Sam Williams described that the Red River in Fulton "spread herself over the entire valley, from bluff to bluff."[278] This flood was the same one that destroyed Jonesboro, the town upriver in what used to be Old Miller County. Other residents remember floods that stretched for miles, causing one boat to founder after having mistaken a cornfield for the river channel. The flood of May 1990 crested at thirty-two feet and created a river that spanned as wide as ten miles in some places.[279] Yet despite all of this trouble, two towns that have tied their fates to the Red River have managed to hang on: Garland City and Fulton.

Garland City's location along the Red River has been both a blessing and a curse. Its location helped it to become an important shipping center for Lafayette County, but it also led to inundating floods. The *WPA Guide to Arkansas* described mud marks on buildings where the water crested and explained that flooding could frequently isolate the town for weeks

Over the years, Fulton, once the "Gateway to the Southwest," has diminished in importance. While the town still has a post office, it no longer has a public school. *From the collections of the Arkansas Historical Commission.*

at a time.[280] What saved Garland City from abandonment was the Cotton Belt, which sliced through town on its way from Texarkana to Lewisville. The railroad built a bridge in 1883.[281] Though the train no longer stops in Garland City, U.S. 82 has proven to be another lifeline for the town. Since Garland City lies at the eastern edge of Miller County, in which alcohol sales are legal, and across from Lafayette County, which is a "dry" county, the town sees many daily visitors.

Fulton manages to survive, too, despite its lack of a downtown business district. It sits proudly, maybe even defiantly, at the confluence of the Red and Little Rivers, the Union Pacific Railroad, U.S. 67 and Interstate 30. While the town is accessible only from the highway, its prime location at the Great Bend has kept the city from disappearing. The strong steel-truss railroad bridge, erected in 1874 and subsequently replaced in 1890, still spans the river between large levees.[282] Still, Fulton has seen terrible destruction brought by the river. A flood in the late 1880s wiped out the entire downtown, and the infamous 1927 flood left its bridge partially destroyed. The high waters that rose in May 1990 could have been disastrous, but the levees protected much of the town. Fulton has become a much sleepier enclave; it no longer sees the hustle and bustle it once did when it served as a frontier town, when a gambler reportedly lost a cotton plantation and the steamboat *Waukesha* in a game of stud poker.[283] However, its proximity to Texarkana allows residents access to work while living in a peaceful old town.

A NEW GREAT BEND

Restoration seems to be the new mantra of southwestern Arkansas. Though commerce and business is still growing, many of the places in southwestern Arkansas are coming of age. Now, instead of building and forgetting, citizens are maintaining and preserving. Museums and parks have appeared all over the region to remind residents and tourists of the important roles southwestern Arkansas played in the state's and even the nation's past.

Washington should be noted for its resilience to survive, because it could have easily succumbed to the modern era of interstates. Bypassed by the railroad, U.S. 67 and Interstate 30, this once-important town of early Arkansas sat quietly along the old military road as a beautiful but decaying time capsule until several people banded together to resurrect the city. Charlean Moss Williams and the members of the Pat Cleburne Chapter of the United Daughters of the Confederacy decided to restore the old town when James H. Pilkington suggested that Washington could become like a Colonial Williamsburg for Arkansas. By this point, however, several buildings, like the old tavern, had been razed or were in a state of major disrepair. By establishing the Community Improvement Club and the Foundation for the Restoration of Pioneer Washington in 1958, work began in earnest to re-create Washington as a tourist destination.[284]

Some of the work had already been done; the 1836 courthouse had been restored in 1929, the first structure in Arkansas to receive funds for preservation. The foundation refurbished the Block-Catts House, home to the first Jewish settler to Arkansas, for its initial project. The historic tavern was rebuilt in 1960 on the location of the original tavern erected by Elijah Stuart. A re-creation of the blacksmith shop, where Jim Bowie supposedly had his famous knife fashioned by James Black, was completed in 1960. Today, inside the former bank sits a weapons museum, and the 1874

The historic tavern at Washington was in bad repair by the 1930s. Washington had lost its place as the Hempstead County seat, and only gravel roads led to the former commercial center. *Courtesy Library of Congress.*

courthouse serves as visitor center. While many homes that were restored are in their original locations, such as the Sanders house, several others have been moved to Washington from nearby communities like Columbus, Marlbrook and Blevins, creating a truly unique outdoor museum. One of the park's prized exhibits is a magnolia tree, planted by Grandison Royston in 1839 and the largest specimen in Arkansas. Other mature trees, like loblolly pines and catalpas, tell the age of this city. In 1973, the town became a historic park administered by the State of Arkansas.[285] The Arkansas Historical Commission expanded its holdings in 1978 by making Washington its southwestern repository.[286] The Southwestern Arkansas Regional Archives (SARA) has become one of the most valuable historical assets in the Red River Valley, in which letters, newspapers, photographs and maps for the region can be found. Initially run by volunteers, the archive has become a professional center of research that sees a stream of visitors daily.

Texarkana has supplanted Washington to become the region's capital city. The Texarkana Museums System tells the story of this fabled city in four separate venues. The Museum of Regional History, located along State Line

Citizens of Washington banded together to preserve the heritage of their beautiful and historically important town. *From the collections of the Arkansas Historical Commission.*

The Arkansas Historical Commission has worked diligently to preserve the history of the Great Bend region, where much evidence has been washed away by floods. *From the collections of the Arkansas Historical Commission.*

Avenue in downtown Texarkana, displays Caddoan artifacts and information on native son Scott Joplin. The Discovery Place Children's Museum sits adjacent to the Museum of Regional History. City lore is recounted in both the Draughon-Moore Ace of Clubs home, which was built in the form of a club to commemorate the owner's lucky hand in a game of cards, and the Patrick Ahern house, a large brick mansion from the turn of the twentieth century. Texarkana-born Ross Perot funded the restoration of the 1934 Saenger Theater in downtown Texarkana, which now hosts ballets, musicals and stage productions.[287] Trains still meet behind Union Station, though the depot has long ago lost its luster. The Texas Eagle, an Amtrak train that connects passengers from Chicago to San Antonio, stops at Texarkana twice daily.

As the birthplace of former U.S. president William Jefferson Clinton, Hope has received a lot of attention. The simple, two-story house that Clinton briefly called home is now a national historic park. Hope has also restored its historic depot, which recently became a station for the Texas Eagle. Ashdown is growing quite steadily thanks to the paper mill, college and the freight trains that still pass through. Its past is preserved through the Little River County Historical Society's dedication to the Two Rivers Museum. Located just off Route 71 (Constitution Avenue), the museum, housed in an old bank, tells the story of inhabitants through well-designed exhibits and one-of-a-kind artifacts.

One of Arkansas' smallest state parks can be visited near the old plantation home of former governor James Conway. Only the family cemetery remains in this small enclave south of Lewisville in Lafayette County. Millwood State Park, north of Ashdown in Little River County, offers recreational opportunities. With its bayous and channels, the lake, created by damming the Little River, may be reminiscent of the way the Red River looked before Captain Henry Shreve removed the Great Raft. The lake is also the site of the former towns of Saline Landing and Saratoga, which was once known as "Cracker's Neck" and is now under water.

Not much remains of most of the towns that figured prominently in the history of the Great Bend region before the Civil War. The commercial buildings of Columbus, Rocky Comfort, Lost Prairie, Long Prairie, Rondo and La Grange are all gone; in some cases, even churches no longer remain. Only the cozy layout of streets indicates that Richmond was once the former seat of Little River County. Wilton's old mercantile exists now as a burnt-out shell. Luckily, Alleene, the county's first incarnation of a capital, still retains its log cabin courthouse. Hempstead County's architectural history was partially wiped out when the Southwest Proving Grounds were built in

Louise Taft documented historic structures in southwestern Arkansas for the federal government. Many of these structures were razed, such as the Pennsylvania truss bridge on U.S. 82 that spanned the Red River at Garland. *Courtesy Library of Congress.*

The Red River ferry between Foreman and New Boston saw its days numbered as a new, free bridge was built in the 1950s. *From the collections of the Arkansas Historical Commission.*

the 1940s, along the old military road between Marlbrook (Blevins), Ozan and Washington; however, a few old buildings, such as a detached kitchen, cotton gin and a tavern, were saved from the wrecking ball when they were moved to Washington State Historic Park.

Many of the original towns have been washed away by floods or ravaged by time, and often, only cemeteries provide reminders of what once was. The same holds true for pre-American locations: most scholars are still unsure of the locations of de la Harpe's fort, the Caddo village depicted by Teran or the old village of Naguatex. Many of the Caddoan burial mounds—which early explorers recounted as being so plentiful—have been obliterated in the landscape, either tilled by farmers or destroyed by grave robbers. A few remain but are often hidden in the underbrush. Without concerted efforts toward preservation and protection, much of this heritage will soon be gone, too.

THE FUTURE OF THE RED RIVER IN SOUTHWESTERN ARKANSAS

In 1995, Lonnie Hazel placed a historic phone call to the U.S. Coast Guard. He informed them that the last ferry operating on the Red River, at Spring Bank, would be decommissioned now that the bridge for Highway 160 had opened.[288] This marked an end of a way of life for the residents in the sparsely inhabited area around Doddridge in southern Miller County, though not everyone mourned it. "A bridge," opined local resident H.T. Williams, "would be…a hundred times better than this old ferry."[289] The Red River had now been completely bypassed in the modern era. Luckily, the citizens of Doddridge raised money and volunteered labor to restore the ferry, which for years sat on the sandy banks just below the junction where the Sulphur River drained into the Red after its days of usefulness were over. It now sits in Doddridge's city park, a monument to an ancient time when rivers were not things to ignore but formidable geographic features that demanded coexistence.[290]

As recently as November 2000, the U.S. Army Corps of Engineers has explored the option of making the Red River navigable once again.[291] Shreveport had done just that in the early 1990s, and it had been born again as an inland commercial port. Why should the Red River not experience the same fate? Since the distant time when humans fashioned communities in the Great Bend region, the river has acted as the lifeblood of the land,

The last ties to southwestern Arkansas' past were severed in 1995, when the Spring Bank Ferry was decommissioned after the Arkansas Highway Department erected a bridge on Highway 160 just south of the Sulphur and Red rivers' confluences. Photo by John Jackson. *Courtesy of Arkansas State Highway and Transportation Department.*

the conduit from which all commerce, connection and interaction stemmed. It has only been very recent—in historical terms, a mere blink of an eye—that the Red River has not figured prominently in the story of southwestern Arkansas. It is time to reclaim the river—to see it as a link to the past and as a powerful force toward the future.

Notes

Chapter 1

1. "Soil Survey by USDA," http://soils.usda.gov/survey/online_surveys/arkansas/millerAR1903/millerAR1903.pdf (accessed August 30, 2013).
2. De la Harpe, *Historical Journal*.
3. Featherstonhaugh, *Excursion through the Slave States*, 120.
4. There is doubt as to whether Caddos and the Quapaws were directly related. William C. Foster, who edited Henri Joutel's journal, points out that Joutel's descriptions of each tribe's language, ceremonies and city building differed considerably.
5. Smith, *Caddo Indians*.
6. De la Harpe, *Historical Journal*.
7. It is now believed by archaeologists that early humans established spiritual centers first before individual villages or cities were founded.
8. Susan Dial and Darrell Creel, "Upper Nasoni," Texas Beyond History, http://www.texasbeyondhistory.net/nasoni/ (accessed June 15, 2013).
9. "Spiro Mounds Artifact Turns Up at Goodwill," *ABC 13 News*, May 4, 2012, http://www.wset.com/story/18147084/spiro-mounds-artifact-turns-up-at-goodwill (accessed June 30, 2013).
10. La Vere, *Caddo Chiefdoms*.
11. Schambach, "The End of the Trail," 78–105.
12. Beasley, *Little River County*, 18.

13. In later years, Caddos would rely on ingesting the peyote bean (part of the movement called the Peyote Cult) to assist them in the visions.
14. Joutel, *La Salle Expedition*.
15. Smith, *Caddo Indians*; La Vere, *Caddo Chiefdoms*.
16. Joutel, *La Salle Expedition*.
17. Smith, *Caddo Indians*.
18. Joutel, *La Salle Expedition*.
19. Ibid., 249.
20. Flores, *Southern Counterpart to Lewis and Clark*, 170.
21. Weber, *Spanish Frontier in North America*, 51.
22. Robertson, *True Relation of the Hardships*.
23. It has been presumed by historians that Moscoso traveled into northern Louisiana, and not southwestern Arkansas, when he visited Naguatex. However, archaeologists have posited the theory that the actual location of their encounters with the Kadohadachos occurred near the Great Bend and in the vicinity of Garland City. See Frank E. Schambach, "The End of the Trail."
24. La Vere, *Caddo Chiefdoms*.
25. Smith, *Caddo Indians*.
26. Ibid.
27. La Vere, *Caddo Chiefdoms*.
28. Smith, *Caddo Indians*.
29. Tyson, *Red River in Southwestern History*; Gleason, *Caddo: A Survey*.
30. The garrison, Fort Saint Louis, was discovered by archaeologists in 1996. The settlement consisted of a main house built from wood salvaged from one of the grounded supply ships and thatched grass houses. The main house also served as a church. The colony existed only for a few short years, as the inhabitants died of disease, starvation or Indian raids.
31. Joutel, *La Salle Expedition*.
32. Ibid.
33. Ibid.
34. Ibid., 245.
35. Ibid., 249.
36. Ibid.
37. Ibid., 252.
38. Joutel, *La Salle Expedition*; De la Harpe, *Historical Journal*.
39. La Vere, *Caddo Chiefdoms*.
40. Tyson, *Red River in Southwestern History*.
41. Ibid.
42. Ibid.

43. De la Harpe, *Historical Journal of the Settlement.*
44. Ibid, 135–36.
45. Ibid., 136–37.
46. Ibid., 139.
47. At this time, New Mexico encompassed today's Texas, Colorado and New Mexico.
48. United States Congressional Record, vol. 2913 and American State Papers, 4:478, 479.
49. Tyson, *Red River in Southwestern History,* 38–39.
50. Ibid., 46.
51. Bolton, "Father Miguel Santa Maria y Silva to the Viceroy July 21, 1774," in *Athanase de Mezieres,* 2:74.
52. Ibid., 78.
53. Bolton, "Frontier Problems" in *Athanase de Mezieres*, 2:136; "Journal of an Expedition up the Red River, 1773–1774" in *Athanase de Mezieres*, 2:83–84.
54. Flores, *Southern Counterpart*, 66–67.
55. Ibid., 127. Dan Flores called the logjam "one of the amazing phenomena of natural North America."
56. Ibid., 154.
57. Ibid., 165.
58. Ibid., 174.
59. Ibid., 176.
60. These red cedar groves are no longer as numerous in the Red River Valley, as most were cut down by railroad and logging companies in the latter part of the nineteenth century.
61. Flores, *Southern Counterpart*, 186. The Caddos called the mountain *Cha'Kam'Na*, and now it is known as Boyd's Hill.
62. Ibid., 194–96.
63. The bluff on the Red River in Bowie County is now called, not coincidentally, Spanish Bluff.
64. Flores, *Southern Counterpart*, 205–6.
65. For thrilling accounts of Randolph B. Marcy's trailblazing, see *The Prairie Traveler: A Hand-Book for Overland Expeditions. With Maps, Illustrations, and Itineraries of the Principal Routes between the Mississippi and the Pacific* (1859). Marcy's discovery of the source of the Red River is recounted in his book, *Exploration of the Red River in the Year 1852 by Randolph B. Marcy; Assisted by George B. McClellan. With Reports on the Natural History of the Country, and Numerous Illustrations* (1853).
66. Carter, *Territorial Papers of Arkansas,* 19:143–44.
67. Ibid., Introduction.

68. The Encyclopedia of Arkansas lists the first location of the Lafayette County Courthouse at Chickaninny Prairie. I have not found maps from the era reflecting this name, however; most point to a place named La Grange.
69. Carter, *Territorial Papers of Arkansas,* 19:70.
70. Lonnie J. White, "Disturbances on the Arkansas-Texas Border, 1827–1831," *Arkansas Historical Quarterly* 19, no. 2 (Summer 1960): 99.
71. Carter, *Territorial Papers of Arkansas,* 20:632.
72. Land filibustering was not unknown to the region. After Aaron Burr, vice president of the United States under Thomas Jefferson, killed Alexander Hamilton in a duel in 1804, Burr visited lands in the West, eventually landing in Louisiana. There he met with James Wilkerson, a senior officer of the army and now known to have been a secret agent for the Spanish government, who conspired with Burr to plan takeovers of Spanish and American lands in the West, with the ultimate goal of forming a separate nation. Wilkinson had an about-face and notified President Jefferson of the proposed filibuster. Burr was tried for treason in the nascent Supreme Court. John Marshall, the longtime chief justice of the Supreme Court who established most of the precedents still used by the courts today, acquitted Burr. Wilkinson may have also tipped off the New Spanish government about the Freeman and Custis expedition.
73. Strickland, "Establishment of Old Miller County," 157.
74. Carter, *Territorial Papers of Arkansas*, 19:565.
75. White, "Disturbances on the Arkansas-Texas Border," 100.
76. "Adams-Onis Treaty," Library of Congress, http://myloc.gov/Exhibitions/EarlyAmericas/AftermathoftheEncounter/CompetitionforEmpire/TheUnitedStatesAnEmergingEmpire/ExhibitObjects/AdamsOnisTreaty.aspx (accessed June 30, 2103).
77. *Arkansas Gazette*, November 17, 1830.
78. Carter, *Territorial Papers of Arkansas,* 21:72–80, 159, 359.
79. Ibid., 339.
80. White, "Disturbances on the Arkansas-Texas border," 109.
81. Carter, *Territorial Papers of Arkansas,* 20:632, 640.
82. Ibid.
83. *Arkansas Gazette,* January 6, 1821.
84. Carter, *Territorial Papers of Arkansas,* 19:244.
85. Ibid., 19:565; Ibid., 20:353.
86. Ibid., 20:92–93.
87. Williams, *Washington, Hempstead County.*
88. Carter, *Territorial Papers of Arkansas,* 20:137–38.
89. Ibid., 19:95–96.

90. Ibid., 20:523–27.
91. Ibid., 20:185.
92. *Arkansas Gazette*, August 30, 1825.
93. Carter, *Territorial Papers of Arkansas,* 20:123.
94. *Arkansas Gazette*, July 15, 1829.
95. Foreman, *Indian Removal.*
96. *Arkansas Gazette*, July 15, 1829.
97. The Choctaws and Chickasaws continued to stream into southwestern Arkansas by 1840, but by then the numbers of migrants were much smaller.
98. Foreman, *Indian Removal*, 54–55.
99. Ibid., 55–56.
100. Carter, *Territorial Papers of Arkansas,* 20:495.
101. Smith and Lehman, *No Land, Only Slaves*.
102. White, *Politics on the Southwestern Frontier.*
103. *Arkansas Gazette*, March 30, 1830.
104. McDowell, Deed Book G.
105. Williams, *Printer's Devil,* 285.
106. Bolton, et. al., *Documentary History of Arkansas*, 69–72.
107. McDowell, Deed Book G.
108. Smith and Lehman, *No Land, Only Slaves,* 6:7, 8, 19, 41; 18:107.
109. Ibid., 6:5, 31, 62; 18: 73.
110. McDowell, Deed Book G.
111. *Arkansas Gazette*, December 1840.
112. Ibid., January 4, 1832.
113. Brown, *Born in Slavery,* vol. 2, part 1: 293, digital ID: 021/295290.
114. Eaton, *Report of the General Superintendent of Freedmen*.
115. Graves, *Born in Slavery,* 10:129, digital ID: 100/131126.
116. *Arkansas Gazette,* January 12, 1842.
117. Ibid., January 4, 1849.
118. Interview of Joe Ray by Ethel Wolfe Garrison, *Bearing Witness*, 143.
119. Ibid., 142.
120. Ibid., 143.
121. Elliot, *Born in Slavery,* vol. 2, part 2: 243, digital ID: 022/239235.
122. Frazier, *Born in Slavery,* vol. 2, part 2: 245, digital ID: 022/348344.
123. Graves, *Born in Slavery*, 10:132.
124. Interview of Sallie Crane by Samuel S. Taylor, *Bearing Witness*, 136–37.
125. Interview of Katie Rowe by Robert Vinson Lackey, *Bearing Witness*, 148.

Chapter 2

126. Featherstonhaugh, *Excursion through the Slave States*, 114.
127. Ibid., 120, 124.
128. Ibid., 120.
129. Ibid., 114.
130. Carter, *Territorial Papers of Arkansas* 21: 900, 1103, 1130, 1145.
131. Ibid., 21: 833.
132. *Arkansas Gazette*, April 5, 1836; Ericson, "Richard Ellis" and "Samuel Carson"; Kemp, "Robert Hamilton" and Albert H. Latimer"; Garver, "Collin McKinney."
133. *Arkansas Gazette*, April 25, 1838.
134. White, "Disturbances on the Arkansas-Texas Border," 109.
135. Smith, *Caddo Indians*.
136. Stevens, *Texas Legation Papers*, 119.
137. Ibid., 259.
138. Ibid., 317.
139. Smith, *Caddo Indians*.
140. Williams, *Printer's Devil*, 182.
141. Williams, *Washington, Hempstead County*.
142. Chandler and Howe, *History of Texarkana*, 60.
143. Williams, *Washington, Hempstead County*.
144. Williams, *Printer's Devil*, 48.
145. Williams, *Washington, Hempstead County*.
146. Williams, *Printer's Devil*, 95; Williams, *Washington, Hempstead County*.
147. Williams, *Printer's Devil*, 195–96.
148. *Arkansas Gazette*, October 17, 1837.
149. "The Blantons of Spring Bank," http://files.usgwarchives.net/ar/miller/history/springb2.txt (accessed November 20, 2013).
150. *Arkansas Gazette*, December 18, 1819.
151. Williams, *Printer's Devil*, 26.
152. Chandler and Howe, *History of Texarkana*, 101.
153. Williams, *Printer's Devil*, 7.
154. Ibid., 22.
155. *Arkansas Gazette*, October 28, 1844.
156. Williams, *Printer's Devil*, 170; Turner, "Columbus, Arkansas."
157. Turner, "Mound Prairie, Arkansas."
158. Ibid., "Saline Landing, Arkansas."
159. *Arkansas Gazette*, August 18, 1841.

160. "The Red River Bridge at Garland City, Arkansas," http://files.usgwarchives.net/ar/miller/history/garland.txt (accessed November 27, 2013).
161. McIver, "Waterbound in Arkansas Part 2," 234–35.
162. Ibid., 225.
163. *Arkansas Gazette*, June 29, 1831.
164. Ibid., July 6, 1831.
165. Carter, *Territorial Papers of Arkansas*, 21:452–53.
166. Ibid., 21:451.
167. *Arkansas Gazette*, October 14, 1847.
168. Ibid., March 21, 1838.
169. Ibid., April 11, 1838.
170. Ibid., January 12, 1839.
171. *Arkansas Gazette*, April 7, 1841; *Washington Telegraph*, 1848; Overton, *History of Texarkana*.
172. Overton, *History of Texarkana*.
173. Bolton, et. al., *Documentary History of Arkansas*, 96.
174. Montgomery, "Hempstead County and the Civil War," 38–46.
175. Ibid., 40.
176. Ibid.
177. Deblack, *With Fire and Sword*, 143.
178. Turner, "Hempstead County's Men," 50.
179. McIver, "Waterbound in Arkansas Part 1," 140.
180. Zorn, "Campaigning in Southern Arkansas," 241.
181. Turner, "Dooley's Ferry," 12–22; Carlson-Dexler, "Crossroads of Conflict." The trenches were not built by slave labor but by the soldiers themselves, as the area had been emptied of slave labor by fleeing plantation owners.
182. Zorn, "Campaigning in Southern Arkansas," 243.
183. Montgomery, "Hempstead County and the Civil War,"40.
184. *Arkansas Gazette*, various accounts, 1862–64.
185. Montgomery, "Hempstead County and the Civil War," 44.

CHAPTER 3

186. Interview of Katie Rowe by Robert Vinson Lackey, *Bearing Witness*, 148–49.
187. Ibid., 150.
188. Indenture Bonds for Hempstead County, Arkansas, 1865–1868, Freedmen's Bureau Online, http://www.freedmensbureau.com/arkansas/arkindenture.htm (accessed October 20, 2013).

189. *Washington Telegraph*, April 21 and April 26, 1872.
190. Quinn, *Born in Slavery*, vol. 2, part 6: 2–4, digital ID: 026/005001.
191. Clayton, *Aftermath of the Civil War in Arkansas*, 99.
192. Ibid., 114–15.
193. Ibid., 60.
194. Ibid., 63.
195. Ibid., 64.
196. Ibid., 224–25.
197. *Washington Telegraph*, n.d.
198. Hanson and Moneyhon, *Historical Atlas of Arkansas*, Map 56.
199. Ibid.
200. Kiser, "The Socialist Party in Arkansas," 119–53.
201. Green, *Grass Roots Socialism*, 250.
202. Auerbach, "Southern Tenant Farmers," 113–31.
203. Bolton et. al, *Documentary History of Arkansas*, 145.
204. *Washington Telegraph*, n.d.
205. Linder, "Pellagra," 1,556–58; Moneyhon, *Arkansas and the New South*, 93–94.
206. Wood, "Development of Arkansas Railroads," 155–93.
207. *New York Sun*, February 2, 1893.
208. Missouri Pacific Railway Company, *Iron Mountain Route*, 10.
209. Condren, "Cairo and Fulton Railroad," *Encyclopedia of Arkansas*.
210. Wood, "Development of Arkansas Railroads," 103–40.
211. Zbinden, "St. Louis Southwestern Railway"; Alison, "St. Louis–San Francisco Railroad"; Duggan, "Narrow Gauge Railroads." *Encyclopedia of Arkansas*.
212. *Arkansas Gazette*, January 8, 1873.
213. Arnold, "Historical Sketch," *Encyclopedia of Arkansas*.
214. "Texarkana Loses," *Red River County Review*.
215. Arnold, "Historical Statement."
216. Cravens, "St. Louis, Arkansas and Texas Railway" and "Texas and St. Louis Railway," *Handbook of Texas Online*.
217. *Arkansas Highways Magazine* 3, no. 1 (January 1926): 10.
218. Arkansas State Highway and Transportation Department, "Texarkana Region Freight Transportation Study (Shipper's Survey), Miller County (September 2008)," http://www.arkansashighways.com/planning_research/statewide_planning/TexarkanaRegionFrtTransportationStudy_ShippersSurveyAll.pdf (accessed October 19, 2013).
219. *WPA Guide*, 197.
220. *Arkansas Gazette*, February 5, 1874.
221. *WPA Guide*, 199.

222. Rowe, *Historic Texarkana,* 48.
223. Southwest Regional Archives, Schools in Miller County, http://www.southwestarchives.dreamhosters.com/schools.php?county=Miller&menu=jonfegjsfhbl (accessed October 20, 2013). The Rosenwald Foundation was founded by Julius Rosenwald, an executive at Sears Roebuck, and Booker T. Washington. In response to underfunding and antipathy toward black education in the Jim Crow South, the Rosenwald Foundation matched the amount of monies raised by communities requesting new school buildings. The foundation was immensely influential, funding over five thousand schools in several states. One of the heaviest concentrations of Rosenwald schools was in the areas surrounding the Great Bend of the Red River.
224. *WPA Guide*, 198.
225. Biffle, "Phantom's Crimes Unavenged," *Dallas Morning News*, 39A.
226. Shriver, *Hope's First Century,* 5.
227. Ibid., 15; *WPA Guide,* 215–16.
228. *Arkansas Gazette*, September 12, 1941.
229. Shriver, *Hope's First Century*, 88.
230. Trey Berry, "Michael Dale Huckabee"; Ernest Dumas, "William Jefferson Clinton." *Encyclopedia of Arkansas.*
231. Williams, *Printer's Devil*, 59.
232. Moneyhon, *Arkansas and the New South*, 112.
233. Schloss, http://blog.roadtrippers.com/the-watermelon-capital-of-the-world/by (accessed August 3, 2013). Hope is not the only town in the United States that claims to be the watermelon capital of the world. Other contenders include Cordele, Georgia; Weatherford, Texas; Green River, Utah; Beardstown, Illinois; Rush Springs, Oklahoma; and Naples, Texas. The clear winner is obviously… undecided.
234. Hope, Arkansas Chamber of Commerce, "History of the Hope Watermelon Festival," http://www.hopechamberofcommerce.com/festival_info.htm (accessed October 22, 2013).
235. Beasley, *Little River County*, 18.
236. Ibid., 19–20.
237. Little River Historical Society, *A History of Ashdown,* 10.
238. Ibid., 157.
239. *Arkansas Gazette*, August 18, 1841.
240. Teske, "Lewisville, Lafayette County."
241. Key, "History of Lewisville," 15–16.
242. Ibid., 16.
243. Ibid., 17.

244. Hanson and Moneyhon, *Historical Atlas of Arkansas*, Maps 36 and 41.
245. Key, "A History of Lewisville," 16.
246. Ibid.
247. Forbes, "Petroleum Industry in Arkansas," 28–40.

CHAPTER 4

248. *WPA Guide*, 216.
249. Ibid., 218.
250. Gatewood, "Arkansas Negroes in the 1890s," 297.
251. McIver, "Waterbound in Arkansas, Part 2." 230–33.
252. Lewis, "Mob Justice," 165.
253. Ibid., 164.
254. "Saw Negro Hanged," *McCurtain Gazette*.
255. Alexander, "White-Robed Reformers," 8–23.
256. Zimmerman, "Convict Lease System in Arkansas," 171–88.
257. Ibid., 185.
258. Williams, *Printer's Devil*, 22.
259. "Historical Review, 1913–2003." *Arkansas State Highway Commission*, 7.
260. Key, "History of Lewisville," 5.
261. *Arkansas Highway Magazine* 3, no. 7 (July 1926): 11.
262. *Arkansas State Highway Commission*, 11–12.
263. Ibid., 13–14.
264. Ibid., 27.
265. Ibid., 22–37.
266. *Arkansas Highway Magazine* 3, no. 8 (August 1926): 8.
267. Ibid., vol. 2, no. 4 (April 1925): 10.
268. Ibid., vol. 3, no. 8 (August 1926): 6.
269. Ibid., vol. 3, no. 10 (October 1929): 15.
270. Ibid., vol. 4, no. 3 (March 1927): 6.
271. Ibid., vol. 1, no. 6 (June 1924): 7.
272. United States Department of Agriculture, Forest Service, "Ouachita National Forest."
273. *WPA Guide*, 321–22.
274. *Arkansas Highway Magazine* 3, no. 9 (September 1926): 6.
275. "Old Hotel on Spirit Lake," *Lafayette Lookback*, 11–12.
276. *Arkansas Highway Magazine* 4, no. 1 (January 1927): 15.
277. *Arkansas Highway Commission*, 101.

278. Williams, *Printer's Devil*, 6.
279. Hancock, "Workers Struggle to Contain River," *Dallas Morning News*, 33A.
280. *WPA Guide*, 372–73.
281. Wood, "Development of Arkansas Railroads, Part II," 160.
282. Ibid., "Development of Arkansas Railroads, Part I,"132.
283. *WPA Guide*, 219.
284. Medaris, *Washington*.
285. Washington State Historic Park, "Tour the Town."
286. "SARA Opens." *Journal of the Hempstead County Historical Society* 2, no. 1 (Spring 1978): 2–4.
287. Simmons, "Mansion That Gambling Built," *Dallas Morning News*.
288. Nilles, "A Piece of History," *Arkansas Highways Magazine*, 6.
289. Schmidt, "Old Ferries Sail on Troubled Waters," *New York Times*.
290. Nilles, "A Piece of History," 5–7.
291. Associated Press Wire Report, "Texarkana Explores Port for Red River," *Dallas Morning News*.

Bibliography

Books

Beasley, Bill. *Little River County*. Foreman, AR: Little River Historical Society, 1975.

Bolton, Charles, C. Fred Williams, Carl Moneyhon, and LeRoy T. Williams, eds. *A Documentary History of Arkansas*. Fayetteville: University of Arkansas Press, 1984.

Bolton, Herbert Eugene, ed. *Athanase de Mezieres and the Louisiana-Texas Frontier, 1768–1780: Documents Published for the First Time, from the Original Spanish and French Manuscripts, Chiefly in the Archives of Spain and Mexico*. Cleveland, OH: The Arthur H. Clark Company, 1914.

Carter, Clarence Edwin, ed. *The Territorial Papers of the United States, Department of State: The Territory of Arkansas, 1819–1825*. Vol. 19. Washington, D.C.: United States Printing Office, 1953.

———. *The Territorial Papers of the United States, Department of State: The Territory of Arkansas, 1825–1829*. Vol. 20. Washington, D.C.: United States Printing Office, 1954.

———. *The Territorial Papers of the United States, Department of State: The Territory of Arkansas, 1829–1836*, Vol. 21. Washington, D.C.: United States Printing Office, 1954.

Chandler, Barbara Overton, and J. Ed Howe. *History of Texarkana and Bowie and Miller Counties, Texas-Arkansas.* Shreveport, LA: J. Ed Howe, Publisher, 1939.

Clayton, Powell. *The Aftermath of the Civil War in Arkansas*. New York: Neale Publishing Company, 1915.

Deblack, Thomas A. *With Fire and Sword: Arkansas, 1864–1874*. Fayetteville: University of Arkansas Press, 2003.

De la Harpe, Jean-Bapstiste. *Historical Journal of the Settlement of the French in Louisiana by Bernard de la Harpe. Maybe Work of Chevalier de Beaurain, Royal Geographer.* Edited and annotated by Glen R. Conrad. Translated by Virginia Koenig and Joan Cain. Lafayette: University of Southwest Louisiana, 1971.

Featherstonhaugh, G.W. *Excursion through the Slave States from Washington on the Potomac to the Frontier of Mexico, with Sketches of Popular Names and Geological Notices*. New York: Negro University Press (1844), 1968.

Flores, Dan L. Flores, ed. *Southern Counterpart to Lewis and Clark: The Freeman and Custis Expedition of 1806.* Norman: University of Oklahoma Press, 1984.

Foreman, Grant. *Indian Removal: The Emigration of the Five Civilized Tribes of Indians*. Norman: University of Oklahoma Press (1932), 1966.

Gleason, Mildred S. *Caddo: A Survey of the Caddo Indians in Northeast Texas and Marion County*. Jefferson, TX: Marion County Historical Society, 1999.

Green, James R. *Grass Roots Socialism: Radical Movements in the Southwest, 1895–1943.* Lafayette: Louisiana State University Press, 1978.

Hanson, Gerald T., and Carl H. Moneyhon. *Historical Atlas of Arkansas*. Norman: University of Oklahoma Press, 1989.

Joutel, Henri. *The La Salle Expedition to Texas: The Journal of Henri Joutel, 1684–1687*. Edited by William C. Foster. Translated by Johanna S. Warren. Austin: Texas State Historical Association, 1998.

Lankford, George E., ed. *Bearing Witness: Memories of Arkansas Slavery Narratives from the 1930s WPA Collections*. Fayetteville: University of Arkansas Press, 2006.

La Vere, David. *The Caddo Chiefdoms: Caddo Economics and Politics, 700–1835.* Lincoln: University of Nebraska Press, 1998.

Little River Historical Society. *A History of Ashdown, Arkansas.* Marceline, MO: Heritage House Publishing, 2006.

McDowell, Linda, comp. "Deed Book G 1838–1847 Hempstead County." In *Black Slaves and Early Freemen of Hempstead County, Arkansas, 1819–1850.* Little Rock: Arkansas Jubilee Inc., 2000.

Medaris, Mary. *Washington, Arkansas: History on the Southwest Trail.* Hope, AR: Etter Printing Company, 1976.

Missouri Pacific Railway Company. *The Iron Mountain Route and Texarkana, the Gateway to Texas.* St. Louis: Missouri Pacific Railway Company, 1896.

Moneyhon, Carl H. *Arkansas and the New South, 1874–1929.* Fayetteville: University of Arkansas Press, 1997.

Robertson, James Alexander, trans. *True Relation of the Hardships Suffered by Governor Hernando de Soto and Certain Portuguese Gentlemen during the Discovery of the Province of Florida, Now Newly Set Forth by a Gentleman of Elvas, 1557.* Jacksonville: Florida State Historical Society, 1933.

Rowe, Beverly J. *Historic Texarkana: An Illustrated History, Commissioned by the Texarkana Museums System.* San Antonio, TX: Historical Publishing Network, 2009.

Schambach, Frank E. "The End of the Trail: Reconstruction of the Route of Hernando de Soto's Army through Southwest Arkansas and East Texas." *The Expedition of Hernando de Soto West of the Mississippi, 1541–1543. Proceedings of the De Soto Symposia, 1988 and 1990.* Edited by Gloria A. Young and Michael P. Hoffman. Fayetteville: University of Arkansas Press, 1993.

Shriver, Harry W., ed. *Hope's First Century: A Commemorative History of Hope, Arkansas 1875–1975.* Hope, AR: Etter Printing Company, 1974.

Smith, Edith, and Vivian Lehman. *No Land, Only Slaves: Slave Conveyances Abstracted from the Deed Books of Lafayette County.* Vol. 6. Balch Springs, TX: 2006.

———. *No Land, Only Slaves: Slave Records Abstracted from the Deed Books of Hempstead County.* Vol. 18. Balch Springs, Texas: 2007.

Smith, F. Todd. *The Caddo Indians: Tribes at the Convergence of Empires, 1542–1854.* College Station: Texas A&M University Press, 1995.

Stevens, Kenneth R., ed. *The Texas Legation Papers, 1836–1845.* Fort Worth: Texas Christian University Press, 2012.

Tyson, Carl Newton. *The Red River in Southwestern History.* Norman: University of Oklahoma Press, 1981.

Weber, David J. *The Spanish Frontier in North America.* New Haven, CT: Yale University Press, 1992.

White, Lonnie J. *Politics on the Southwestern Frontier, Arkansas Territory 1819–1836.* Memphis, TN: Memphis State University Press, 1964.

Williams, Charlean Moss. *Washington, Hempstead County, Arkansas: Gateway to Texas, Confederate Capital 1863.* Houston, TX: Anson Jones Press, 1951.

Williams, Sam. *Printer's Devil. Memorabilia. Some Ante-bellum Reminisces of Hempstead County, Arkansas. Embracing Pictures, Social Life, Personal Sketches, Political Annals and Anecdotes of Characters and Events.* Edited by Mary Medearis. Hope, AR: Etter Printing Company, 1979.

JOURNAL ARTICLES

Alexander, Charles C. "White-Robed Reformers: The Ku Klux Klan Comes to Arkansas, 1921–1922." *Arkansas Historical Quarterly* 22, no. 1 (Spring 1963): 8–23.

Arnold, W.H., Sr. "Historical Sketch Relating to the Establishment of State Line in Arkansas." *Arkansas Historical Quarterly* 5 (1946).

———. "Historical Statement by W.H. Arnold of Texarkana, Arkansas" (February 7, 1917), *Arkansas Historical Quarterly* 5 (1946).

Auerbach, Jerold S. "Southern Tenant Farmers: Socialist Critics of the New Deal." *Arkansas Historical Quarterly* 27, no. 2 (Summer 1968): 113–31.

Carlson-Dexler, Carl G. "Crossroads of Conflict: Archeology at Dooley's Ferry." http://www.academia.edu/1534109/Crossroads_of_Conflict_Archaeology_at_Dooleys_Ferry_Hempstead_County_Arkansas.

Forbes, Gerald. "Brief History of the Petroleum Industry in Arkansas." *Arkansas Historical Quarterly* 1, no. 1 (March 1942): 28–40.

Gatewood, William. "Arkansas Negroes in the 1890s: Documents." *Arkansas Historical Quarterly* 33, no. 4 (Winter 1974): 293–325.

Key, Frank. "A History of Lewisville, Arkansas from 1893 through 1913." *Lafayette Lookback* 2, no. 1 (1985): 15–23.

———. "A History of Lewisville, Arkansas Part II." *Lafayette Lookback* 2, no. 1 (1985): 3–8.

Kiser, G. Gregory. "The Socialist Party in Arkansas, 1900–1912." *Arkansas Historical Quarterly* 40, no. 2 (Summer 1981): 119–53.

Lewis, Todd E. "Mob Justice in the American Congo: Judge Lynch in Arkansas during the Decade after World War I." *Arkansas Historical Quarterly* 52, no. 2 (Summer 1993): 165.

Linder, C.H. "Pellagra: Prevalence and Geographic Distribution in Arkansas, Oklahoma and Texas." *Public Health Reports, 1896–1970* 28 no. 3 (July 1913): 1,556–58.

McIver, H.M. "Waterbound in Arkansas Part 1 by H.M. McIver, Texarkana Engineer and Son of a Texas Ranger Who Lived in Rocky Comfort as a Kid." *Arkansas Historical Quarterly* 14, no. 2 (Summer 1955): 134–160.

———. "Waterbound in Arkansas Part 2." *Arkansas Historical Quarterly* 14, no. 3 (Autumn 1955): 225–51.

Montgomery, Don. "Hempstead County and the Civil War: The Home Front." *Journal of the Hempstead County Historical Society* (Winter 2001): 38–46.

"Old Hotel on Spirit Lake." *Lafayette Lookback* 2, no. 2 (1986): 11–12.

"SARA Opens." *Journal of the Hempstead County Historical Society* 2, no. 1 (Spring 1978): 2–4.

Strickland, Rex W. "Establishment of Old Miller County, Arkansas Territory, Chapter 2." *Chronicles of Oklahoma* 18, no. 2 (June 1940): 154–70.

Turner, Mary Nell. "Columbus, Arkansas." *Journal of the Hempstead County Historical Society* 15 (1999).

———. "Dooley's Ferry on Red River: A Brief History." *Journal of the Hempstead County Historical Society* 13 (1994): 12–22.

———. "Mound Prairie, Arkansas." *Journal of the Hempstead County Historical Society* 15 (1999).

———. "Saline Landing, Arkansas." *Journal of the Hempstead County Historical Society* 15 (1999).

Turner, Mary Nell, ed. "Hempstead County's Men Beat Their Plowshares into Swords: Excerpts from Journals and Letters." *Journal of the Hempstead County Historical Society* (Winter 2001): 47–57.

White, Lonnie J. "Disturbances on the Arkansas-Texas Border, 1827–1831." *Arkansas Historical Quarterly* 19, no. 2 (Summer 1960): 95–110.

Wood, Stephen E. "Development of Arkansas Railroads, Part I: Early Interest and Activities." *Arkansas Historical Quarterly* 7, no. 2 (Summer 1948): 103–140.

———."Development of Arkansas Railroads, Part II: The Great Railroad Boom." *Arkansas Historical Quarterly* 7, no. 3 (Autumn 1948): 155–93.

Zimmerman, Jane. "The Convict Lease System in Arkansas and the Fight for Abolition." *Arkansas Historical Quarterly* 8, no. 3 (Autumn 1949): 171–88.

Zorn, Roman J. "Campaigning in Southern Arkansas, a Memoir by C.T. Anderson." *Arkansas Historical Quarterly* 8, no. 3 (Autumn 1999): 240–44.

LIBRARY OF CONGRESS

"Adams-Onis Treaty." http://myloc.gov/Exhibitions/EarlyAmericas/AftermathoftheEncounter/CompetitionforEmpire/TheUnitedStatesAnEmergingEmpire/ExhibitObjects/AdamsOnisTreaty.aspx.

Born in Slavery: Slave Narratives from the Federal Writer's Project, 1936–1938.
Lewis Brown, vol. 2, part 1: 290–98. Digital ID: 021/295290.
John Elliot, vol. 2, Part 2: 235–40. Digital ID: 022/239235.

Doc Quinn, vol. 2, Part 6: 1–5. Digital ID: 026/005001.
Tyler Frazier, vol. 2, Part 2: 344–45. Digital ID: 022/348344.

NEWSPAPERS, MAGAZINES AND NEWS STATIONS

ABC News 13, Buffalo, New York. "Spiro Mounds Artifact Turns Up at Goodwill," May 4, 2012. http://www.wset.com/story/18147084/spiro-mounds-artifact-turns-up-at-goodwill (accessed June 30, 2013).

Arkansas Gazette. Index and microfilm rolls at the Arkansas Historical Commission Library, Little Rock, Arkansas.

Arkansas Highways Magazine. http://www.arkansashighways.com.

Associated Press Wire Report. "Texarkana Explores Port for Red River." *Dallas Morning News*, November 19, 2000.

Biffle, Kent. "Phantom's Crimes Unavenged: The Sex-Crazy, Hooded Killer Who Haunted Lovers' Lanes Was Never Unmasked." *Dallas Morning News*, January 5, 2003.

Hancock, Lee. "Workers Struggle to Contain River—Parts of Levee Like Jelly." *Dallas Morning News*, May 10, 1990.

Nilles, David. "A Piece of History Comes Home to Doddridge." *Arkansas Highways Magazine*, July 2013, 5–7.

"Saw Negro Hanged by Mob Down at Hope—But There Was No Hope for Negro After Mob Took Charge." *McCurtain Gazette* (Idabel, OK) 15, no. 8, March 19, 1921.

Schmidt, William E. "In Arkansas, Old Ferries Sail on Troubled Waters." *New York Times*, August 31, 1986.

Simmons, Jean. "In Texarkana, the Mansion That Gambling Built." *Dallas Morning News*, November 12, 1989.

"Texarkana Loses by a Small Figure: Unofficial Returns Show 344 Votes Needed to Move Courthouse." *Red River County Review* 5, no. 75, first edition. March 25, 1926.

Washington Telegraph. Index to editions at Southwestern Arkansas Regional Archives, Washington, Arkansas.

ONLINE RESOURCES

Alison, Charles Y. "St. Louis–San Francisco Railroad." *Encyclopedia of Arkansas*. www.encylopediaofarkansas.net.

Berry, Trey. "Michael Dale Huckabee." *Encyclopedia of Arkansas*. www.encylopediaofarkansas.net.

Condren, S. Michael. "Cairo and Fulton Railroad." *Encyclopedia of Arkansas*. www.encylopediaofarkansas.net.

Cravens, Chris. "St. Louis, Arkansas and Texas Railway" and "Texas and St. Louis Railway." *Handbook of Texas Online*. www.tshaonline.org/handbook/online.

Dial, Susan, and Darrell Creel. "Upper Nasoni." Texas Beyond History. www.texasbeyondhistory.net.

Duggan, Tom. "Narrow Gauge Railroads." *Encyclopedia of Arkansas*. www.encylopediaofarkansas.net.

Dumas, Ernest. "William Jefferson Clinton." *Encyclopedia of Arkansas*. www.encylopediaofarkansas.net.

Ericson, Joe E. "Richard Ellis" and "Samuel Carson." *Handbook of Texas Online*. www.tshaonline.org/handbook/online.

Freedmen's Bureau Online. "Indenture Bonds for Hempstead County, Arkansas, 1865–1868." www.freedmensbureau.com.

Garver, Lois. "Collin McKinney." *Handbook of Texas Online*. www.tshaonline.org/handbook/online.

Hope Chamber of Commerce. "History of the Hope Watermelon Festival." www.hopechamberofcommerce.com.

Kemp, L.W. "Albert H. Latimer" and "Robert Hamilton." *Handbook of Texas Online*. www.tshaonline.org/handbook/online.

Schloss, Signe. "Watermelon Capital of the World." Road Tripper Blog. www.blog.roadtrippers.com.

Southwest Regional Archives. "Schools in Miller County." www.southwestarchives.dreamhosters.com.

US GenWeb Archives. "The Blantons of Spring Bank." files.usgwarchives.net.

———. "The Red River Bridge at Garland City, Arkansas." files.usgwarchives.net.

Teske, Steven. "Lewisville, Lafayette County." *Encyclopedia of Arkansas*. www.encyclopediaofarkansas.net

Zbinden, Van. "St. Louis Southwestern Railway." *Encyclopedia of Arkansas*. www.encylopediaofarkansas.net.

ARKANSAS STATE AGENCIES AND UNITED STATES AGENCIES

Arkansas State Highway and Transportation Department. "Texarkana Region Freight Transportation Study Shipper's Survey), Miller County." September 2008.

Arkansas State Highway Commission. "Historical Review, 1913–2003." *Arkansas State Highway Commission and Arkansas State Highway and Transportation Department*, April 2004.

Eaton, John. *Report of the General Superintendent of Freedmen, Department of the Tennessee and State of Arkansas, for 1864, Volume 1 by John Eaton*. (Memphis: 1864). Facsimile copy.

United States Department of Agriculture. "Soil Survey of Miller County, Arkansas." www.usda.gov.

United States Department of Agriculture, Forest Service. "Ouachita National Forest." www.fs.usda.gov.

Washington State Historic Park. "Tour the Town." www.historicwashingtonstatepark.com.

The WPA Guide to 1930s Arkansas, Compiled by Workers of the Writers' Program of the Work Projects Administration in the State of Arkansas with a New Introduction by Elliot West. Lawrence: University of Kansas Press (1941), 1987.

PHOTOGRAPHS AND MAPS

Arkansas Historical Commission
Arkansas State Highway Department
Dallas Public Library
Library of Congress

Index

A

B

C

G

H

I

J

K

L

M

N

O

P

About the Author

Robin Cole-Jett teaches history at North Central Texas College. Holding two master's degrees from the University of North Texas and Texas Woman's University, she is also the author of three books: *Traveling History Up the Cattle Trails*, *Traveling History with Bonnie and Clyde* and *Images of America: Lewsiville, Texas*. Her research interests in the Red River of the south manifest themselves in her website, Red River Historian.com—History Where the South Meets the West. Robin lives in Highland Village, Texas, where, in addition to teaching, she conducts Bonnie and Clyde tours and gives lectures on early schools, explorations and ghost towns in the Red River Valley.